Lecture Notes in Computer Scie

T0250835

Commenced Publication in 1973
Founding and Former Series Editors:
Gerhard Goos, Juris Hartmanis, and Jan van Leeuwen

Editorial Board

David Hutchison
Lancaster University, UK

Takeo Kanade
Carnegie Mellon University, Pittsburgh, PA, USA

Josef Kittler
University of Surrey, Guildford, UK

Jon M. Kleinberg
Cornell University, Ithaca, NY, USA

Friedemann Mattern
ETH Zurich, Switzerland

John C. Mitchell
Stanford University, CA, USA

Moni Naor
Weizmann Institute of Science, Rehovot, Israel

Oscar Nierstrasz
University of Bern, Switzerland

C. Pandu Rangan
Indian Institute of Technology, Madras, India

Bernhard Steffen
University of Dortmund, Germany

Madhu Sudan
Massachusetts Institute of Technology, MA, USA

Demetri Terzopoulos
University of California, Los Angeles, CA, USA

Doug Tygar
University of California, Berkeley, CA, USA

Moshe Y. Vardi
Rice University, Houston, TX, USA

Gerhard Weikum
Max-Planck Institute of Computer Science, Saarbruecken, Germany

Miroslaw Malek   Manfred Reitenspieß
Aad van Moorsel (Eds.)

Service Availability

4th International Service Availability
Symposium, ISAS 2007
Durham, NH, USA, May 21-22, 2007
Proceedings

 Springer

Volume Editors

Miroslaw Malek
Humboldt-Universität zu Berlin
Institut für Informatik, Rechnerorganisation und Kommunikation
Rudower Chaussee 25, 12489 Berlin, Germany
E-mail: malek@informatik.hu-berlin.de

Manfred Reitenspieß
Fujitsu Siemens Computers
Domagkstr. 28, D-80807 München, Germany
E-mail: manfred.reitenspiess@fujitsu-siemens.com

Aad van Moorsel
Newcastle University
School of Computing Science
NE1 7RU, Newcastle upon Tyne, UK
E-mail: aad.vanmoorsel@newcastle.ac.uk

Library of Congress Control Number: 2007927310

CR Subject Classification (1998): C.2, H.4, H.3, I.2.11, D.2, H.5, K.4.4, K.6

LNCS Sublibrary: SL 3 – Information Systems and Application, incl. Internet/Web and HCI

ISSN	0302-9743
ISBN-10	3-540-72735-3 Springer Berlin Heidelberg New York
ISBN-13	978-3-540-72735-4 Springer Berlin Heidelberg New York

This work is subject to copyright. All rights are reserved, whether the whole or part of the material is concerned, specifically the rights of translation, reprinting, re-use of illustrations, recitation, broadcasting, reproduction on microfilms or in any other way, and storage in data banks. Duplication of this publication or parts thereof is permitted only under the provisions of the German Copyright Law of September 9, 1965, in its current version, and permission for use must always be obtained from Springer. Violations are liable to prosecution under the German Copyright Law.

Springer is a part of Springer Science+Business Media

springer.com

© Springer-Verlag Berlin Heidelberg 2007

Typesetting: Camera-ready by author, data conversion by Scientific Publishing Services, Chennai, India
Printed on acid-free paper   SPIN: 12068531   06/3180   5 4 3 2 1 0

Preface

Program Chairs' Message

The 4th International Service Availability Symposium (ISAS 2007) continued with the tradition of its predecessors by bringing together researchers and practitioners from both academia and industry to address the problems of service availability. The unique characteristic of a strong academic and industrial partnership was vividly reflected in this year's event, from the Organizing Committee to the contributions and the participants. Recognizing the value of broadening the scope of ISAS 2007, we included new topic areas that cover model-driven design and human factors.

We received a total of 25 submissions, each of which was thoroughly reviewed by at least three members of the Program Committee. Due to the limited time allocated for the symposium, many worthwhile manuscripts unfortunately did not make it into the final program. Our sincere thanks go to the Program Committee for conducting a vigorous review process in a rather tight time schedule. The detailed reviews and their generous comments have shaped the contributions into an excellent program.

Supported by EU project HIDENETS, we organized a half-day post-symposium tutorial that connected the research contributions of the workshop with the industrial standardization efforts in the SA Forum. We are grateful to András Kövi for providing a tutorial on "Principles of HA Design for Planners."

We are indebted to the University of New Hampshire for providing the support and resources needed for hosting ISAS 2007 in Durham, New Hampshire. The local arrangement team led by Scott Valcourt did a tremendous job of assisting the planning and organizing and coordinating all the local activities. We would also like to acknowledge the involvement and support given by the Service Availability Forum and GI/ITG Technical Committee on "Dependability and Fault Tolerance."

We hope that you will find many contributions that are of interests to you, in these proceedings.

May 2007

Aad van Moorsel
Asif Naseem

Organization

ISAS 2007 was organized by the University of New Hampshire, in cooperation with GI (German Computer Society) and Service Availability Forum.

ISAS 2007 Steering Committee

F. Tam (Nokia, Finland)
M. Reitenspieß (Fujitsu Siemens Computers, Germany)
D. Penkler (HP, France)
M. Malek (Humboldt University, Germany)
T. Dohi (Hiroshima University, Japan)
S. Benlarbi (Alcatel, Canada)

ISAS 2007 Organizing Committee

Local Chair

Scott Valcourt (University of New Hampshire, USA)

Program Co-chairs

Aad van Moorsel (University of Newcastle, UK)
Asif Naseem (GoAhead, USA)

ISAS 2007 Reviewers

A. Avritzer (Siemens, USA)
S. Benlarbi (Alcatel, Canada)
A. Birolini (ETH, Switzerland)

S. Bruening (Humboldt University, Germany)
J. Carrasco (UPC, Spain)
Y. Chen (University of Newcastle, UK)
C. Fetzer (TU Dresden, Germany)
M. Garzia (Microsoft, USA)
S. Gokhale (University of Connecticut, USA)
B. Haverkort (University of Twente, The Netherlands)
Y. Kakuda (Hiroshima CU, Japan)
V. Loll (Nokia, Denmark)

D. Bakken (Washington S., USA)
K. Birman (Cornell, USA)
A. Bondavalli (University of Florence, Italy)
A. Burghelea (Cisco, USA)

I. Chen (Virginia Tech, USA)
T. Dohi (Hiroshima University, Japan)
R. Fricks (Motorola, USA)
A. Gokhale (Vanderbilt, USA)
M. Hasan (Cisco, USA)

S. Hunter (IBM, USA)

A. Krings (University of Idaho, USA)
X. Lu (Tokyo I. Tech., Japan)

M. Lyu (Chinese University, Hong Kong)

R. Mansharamani (Tata, India)
K. Mori (Tokyo I. Tech., Japan)
P. Murray (HP, UK)

D. Penkler (HP, France)
A. Rodriguez-Vargas (Siemens, Germany)

H. Sun (Sun Microsystems, USA)
H. Szczerbicka (University of Hannover, Germany)
F. Tam (Nokia, Finland)
B. Vashaw (IBM, USA)
D. Wang (Duke University, USA)

A. Wolski (Solid Tech., Finland)
S. Yajnik (Avaya, USA)

M. Malek (Humboldt University, Germany)
V. Mendiratta (Lucent, USA)
B. Murphy (Microsoft, UK)
E. Nett (University of Magdeburg, Germany)
A. Rindos (IBM, USA)
A. Romanovsky (University of Newcastle, UK)
N. Suri (TU Darmstadt, Germany)
S. Tai (IBM, USA)

K. Trivedi (Duke University, USA)
E. Vollset (Cornell, USA)
K. Wolter (Humboldt University, Germany)
J. Xu (University of Leeds, UK)

Table of Contents

Middleware

Software Systems

Modeling and Analysis

Model-Driven Development and Human Engineering

Autonomous Decentralized System for Service Assurance and Its Application

Kinji Mori

Department of Computer Science, Tokyo Institute of Technology,
2-12-1 Ookayama, Meguro, Tokyo 152-8552, Japan
Tel.: +81-3-5734-2664, Fax: +81-3-5734-2510
mori@cs.titech.ac.jp

Abstract. The market and users requirements have been rapidly changing and diversified. Under these heterogeneous and dynamic situations, not only the system structure itself, but also the accessible information services would be changed constantly. Therefor, the integration of wired and wireless devices, control and information systems to achieve real-time, high-performance and high-reliability for heterogeneous service provision and utilization is becoming more and more important. The Autonomous Decentralized System (ADS) has been proposed for resolving the on-line property to achieve the step-by-step expansion, maintenance and fault-propagation prevention for high-assurance. In this paper, the ADS architecture, autonomous community and application example in the IC card system are discussed.

Keywords: Autonomous Decentralized System, Service Assurance, Autonomous Community, real-time, high-performance.

1 Introduction

The enormous growth of mobile and embedded devices in ubiquitous computing environment and their interaction with human beings offers rapidly evolving and frequently accessed information spaces for anyone, anywhere, anytime [1] [2]. Heterogeneous distributed architectures are required for such systems, where devices are interconnected by various types of communication links, and multiple tasks are concurrently run on the system. These devices may be battery constrained or subject to hostile environments, so communication noise and individual device failure will be a regular or common event. In addition, the configuration devices will frequently change in terms of mobility and task details. Finally, because these devices interact with the physical environment, they, and the network as a whole, will experience a significant range of service content dynamics [3] [4]. However, the conventional architecture is either overdesigned or fails to meet the specified constraints. Therefore, finding an effective architecture to meet the heterogeneous requirements under this dynamic changing environment is necessary.

M. Malek et al.(Eds.): ISAS 2007, LNCS 4526, pp. 1–8, 2007.
© Springer-Verlag Berlin Heidelberg 2007

As the breakthrough over the conventional systems, Autonomous Decentralized System (ADS) has been proposed in 1977 [5] [6]. An autonomous decentralized system is defined as such a living thing which is composed of largely autonomous and decentralized components (subsystems). Their technologies have been developed in the various fields of transportation, factory automation, utility management, satellite on-board control, newspaper printing factory, information services, e-commerce, community service, and so on.

In this paper, the ADS concept and architecture are discussed and the application based on the autonomous community for IC card ticket system: Suica is shown to be effectively operated.

2 Requirements

2.1 Application Needs

Convergence of computer and communication technologies has created demand for ever-increasing levels of assurance. Now network users are demanding and expecting continuous delivery of services: they want always-on services and connections that are maintained without any internal system faults or failures [7]. And in order to maintain and attract new customers, service providers must offer personalized and efficient end-user service. The service assurance is characterized by the following properties:

- **Heterogeneity:** Systems react continuously to their environment at a speed imposed by the environment which lead often real-time capabilities. Reliability, robustness and safety constraints derive from situations where service continuation is impossible. Under the ubiquitous and sensed networked environment, various applications are integrated to achieve multiple requirements, but their requirement levels may be heterogeneous.
- **Adaptability:** The time for the design and commercialization of a system have to be done considering that the users requirements that derive from general trends in society related to aspects like individualization, globalization, mobility, fashion, etc., are always changing. Increasing individualization leads to more diversity in products and services, and therefore to the need for more adaptability in design. Growing needs for continuous service utilization and provision leads to online maintenance and testing.

2.2 System Needs

The service assurance represents a shift from a technology-centric orientation to a customer-centric one in system design [8]. It includes providing high availability, but adds the requirements of service continuity and realtime. Neither scheduled maintenance nor unexpected failure ought to prevent or disrupt provision of service to a customer.

A service assurance solution requires a system be highly available and provide continuity of service. For satisfying the application needs of heterogeneity and adaptability, reliability, robustness and safety constraints derive from situations where service continuation is impossible and a certain degree of adaptive behavior, configuring and organization should be possible.

Application needs and technological background make more requirements of online expansion, fault-tolerance and online maintenance for the system. The online property is one of the major requirements of service assurance system. Current hardware/software design and integration technologies must be developed in order to cope with such challenges. The individualization in the users preferences will force that the new devices must be designed under the metrics of collaborative adaptive systems. The non-stop service utilization and provision will impose constraints on the design and implementation of systems for supporting online maintenance and testing. Moreover, due to the gigantic size of the future systems, the design and implementation will be done on a step by step development considerations.

3   Autonomous Decentralized System

3.1   ADS Concept

Autonomous Decentralized System (ADS) has been proposed to resolve the online property of on-line expansion, on-line maintenance and fault tolerance in a system, which means that the system can continue operation during partial expansion, maintenance and at the time of a partial fault [6]. The ADS is defined as the characteristics that each subsystem can control itself and coordinate with all of the other operating subsystems. Therefore the following two properties must be satisfied by each subsystem: Autonomous Controllability and Autonomous Coordinability.

3.2   ADS Architecture

Each subsystem has its own management system, the Autonomous Control Processor (ACP) to manage itself and coordinate with the others. The subsystem including its application software modules and ACP is an autonomous unit called "Atom". The self-contained subsystems including their respective ACPs are integrated into a system. In the ADS, all of the subsystems are connected only through the Data Field (DF); all data is broadcasted into the DF and the data itself logically circulates in the DF (see Figure 1). The data moves around the application modules in the Atom and the DF in the Atom is called the Atom Data Field (ADF). In the DF, each data is attached with its "content code" which is uniquely defined with respect to the content of the data. To protect the operation of the subsystems from variation in the system, each subsystem broadcasts a message containing the content code instead of the receivers address. The application module is specified only by input and output content codes, and it is executed by the ACP only when all of the necessary data with the proper input content codes is received from the DF (Data-Driven Mechanism). The necessary content codes for the Atom are determined dependently on the application functions within it.

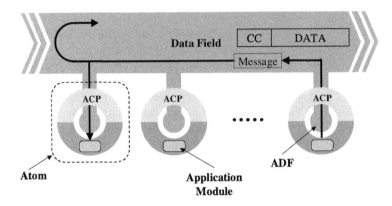

Fig. 1. ADS Architecture

4   Autonomous Community

Community services, which are extended from situation-aware services like location-based services. Community is constructed among the users, who have common preference or are in similar situation, and where services characterized by right now, right here and right me are provided and utilized in accordance with the cooperation of users. The widespread deployment and use of wireless data communications have made the location-based services possible to achieve these requirements.

Under the evolving market, users require the continuous and timely services based on their preference and current location. For effective service provision, service providers need the current requirement of the Local Majority. Service providers (SPs) require for carrying out the marketing on real-time and collect users' requirements to provide most suitable service for local majority at each time. Users' request should be sent to appropriate service providers according to their preference and location. The system that generates the service according to the situation on each occasion by collecting demands of users on real time in local area and provides suitable users with information to achieve real time and availability requirements.

Autonomous Community System consists of autonomous subsystems. Community, which is a dynamic group defined by a service, is created among these entities. In this community, entities that join a community are called members. Communication and process among members in the community realize the community service.

5   Application

5.1   Autonomous Decentralized IC Card Ticket System

A new real-time application of service assurance which has successfully been developed and implemented utilizing ADS architecture and Autonomous

Community concept is the IC card ticket system (Suica), introduced by East Japan Railway Company in November 2001 [9]. This world-wide largest control and information system is an integrated combination of wired and wireless systems, where a contactless IC card communicates by wireless with automatic fare collection devices (terminals) such as automatic fare collection system (AFCS), and the terminals communicate by wired with data collection servers. Nowadays, the integration of control and information systems is becoming more and more important. This integration not only make it possible for message to be exchanged between control and information system, but also makes it possible to create a adaptive integrated system that can satisfy the heterogeneous requirements of applications. The current number of card holders is approximately about 30 million and the number of transactions that are processed daily is in the order of 8 million [10]. And from March 18, 2007, this system is not only available for train system, but also available for other public transport systems.

The gate control and transaction process have been integrated in this system. It is necessary for terminal AFCS devices to provide high performance and high reliability because of the nature of railway transportation service. However, it was difficult to realize both in the IC card ticket system because the short time and noise of wireless communication. For these reasons, technologies and applications that can meet these requirements have been introduced. In the system, IC cards and terminals are designed as autonomous subsystems and configured in autonomous decentralized architecture. As shown in figure 2, the system consists of three different sub-communities (Data Field) with various time ranges. These time ranges of data flows are varied according to needs and aims of both

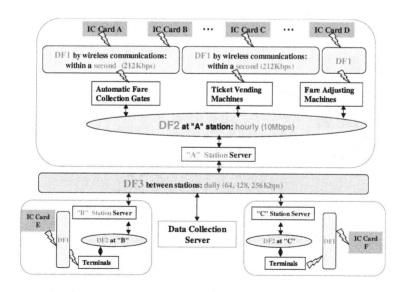

Fig. 2. Different Data Fields architecture

high performance and reliability. In the DF1, terminals use wireless communication with IC cards. The terminals and station server are linked to the station LAN and work on autonomous decentralized process through the DF2. Each terminal operates autonomously and failures at some terminals do not influence on the others. In addition, station servers are connected to a data collection server through the DF3, so if trouble occurs, the trouble does not expand into the whole system. Therefore, passengers can use all functions, derived from the Data Field, when they move between the stations.

5.2   Autonomous Decentralized Process

The development of the wireless IC card ticket system is concretely aimed at the high performance because it is very important to let passengers pass through gates as smoothly as possible, especially during the rush hours. As a result, the process must be finished within 200ms. Figure 3 shows the outline of the technology to process data at high-speed at the automatic gate for fare calculation. The passenger with a Suica commuter pass has to do is to pass this Suica card over the reader/writer (R/W) at the ticket gate, and the necessary fare adjustment is automatically carried out. Since long time is necessary for complicated calculations, a technology that adapt to the particular users situation by sensing mobility depended Autonomous Decentralized Algorithm is proposed. In this algorithm, the fares are autonomously calculated in two processes: the Pre-boarding Process upon entrance and the Post-boarding Process upon exit, followed by the autonomous cooperative process. This algorithm has succeeded in shortening each processing time.

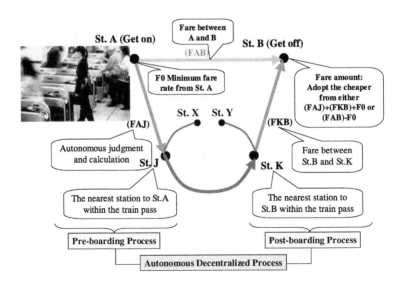

Fig. 3. Autonomous decentralized process

5.3   Heterogeneous Data Fields

Figure 4 shows the data process among heterogeneous DFs which improve the through rate of passengers even in data inconsistent conditions. The R/W sensor updates its data when it receives a completed signal from an IC card. This signal is transmitted near the boarder of the communication area, so that the process is not always completed successfully due to the noise of wireless communication. In this case, the data through the R/W sensor are not updated, though the ones in the card are updated. As a result, the data inconsistency will happen and we call this problem as data lack.

To prevent this problem, Autonomous Decentralized Data Consistency technology is proposed. The inconsistent data can be recovered by using the autonomous decentralized architecture with different DFs. The inconsistent data in the R/W are saved as temporary data in the data collection server. If the next processes are completed normally, the consistency of normal data sent to the data collection server and the previously saved data are checked. And the data consistency can be logically completed based on the normal data.

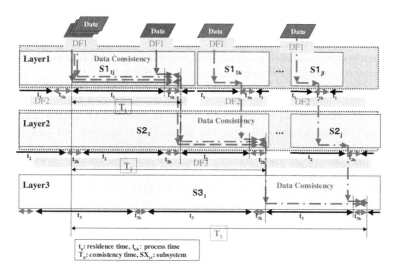

Fig. 4. Heterogeneous DFs process

6   Conclusions

Under the recent severe economic situation, the business in the various fields has been changing to produce new products and to supply new services with high assurance. Moreover the life-cycle of these products and services have been getting short. As the technological trends, the openness and the down-sizing phenomena have been in progress, and the system is constructed by the multi-vender's machines.

The ADS concept and autonomous community are explained under the backgrounds not for the resource utilization, but for the easy-to-use and the easy-to-construct of the computing and controlling systems for service assurance. This architecture shows that there exists no master and no direction among subsystems, and then the software productivity is much improved by building block manner of autonomous software modules. Moreover the real-time application of the autonomous community is described and its validity has been verified.

References

1. Michael N. Huhns and Munindar P. Singh: Service-Oriented Computing: Key Concepts and Principles. IEEE Internet Computing, vol.1 (2005) 75-81
2. David Oppenheimer and David A. Patterson: Architecture and Dependability of Large-Scale Internet Services. IEEE Internet Computing, vol.9 (2002) 41-49
3. P. Bellavista and A. Corradi and C. Stefanelli: The Ubiquitous Provisioning of Internet Services to Portable Devices. IEEE Pervasive Computing, vol.1, no.3. (2002) 81-87
4. H. Schulzrinne and X. Wu and S. Sidiroglou and S. Berger: Ubiquitous computing in home networks. IEEE Communications Magazine, vol.41, no.11. (2003) 128-135
5. K. Mori and et al: Proposition of autonomous decentralized concept. Trans. IEE of Japan, vol.104C, no.12. (1984) 303-340
6. K. Mori: Autonomous Decentralized Systems: concepts, data field architecture and future trends. Proc. IEEE Conf. on ISADS. (1993) 28-34
7. Roger Cummings: The Evolution of Information Assurance. IEEE Computer, vol.12 (2002) 65-72
8. Gerardo Canfora and Massimiliano Di Penta: Testing Services and Service-Centric Systems: Challenges and Opportunities. IEEE IT Professional, vol.3 (2006) 10-17
9. A. Shiibashi: Autonomous decentralized high-speed processing technology and the application in an integrated IC card fixed-line and wireless system. IEICE, vol.88-D, no.12. (2005) 2699-2707
10. A. Shiibashi and K. Mori: Autonomous decentralized data consistency for high-assurance embedded system. Intl. Scientific Journal of Computing, vol.4, no.2. (2006)

A Message Oriented Middleware Solution Enabling Non-repudiation Evidence Generation for Reliable Web Services

Simon Parkin[1], David Ingham[2], and Graham Morgan[1]

[1] School of Computing Science, University of Newcastle, NE1 7RU, UK
[2] Arjuna Technologies Ltd., Newcastle upon Tyne, NE1 7RU, UK
{S.E.Parkin,Graham.Morgan}@newcastle.ac.uk,
dave.ingham@arjuna.com

Abstract. The paper describes an approach to providing reliable message passing together with mechanisms for enforcing non-repudiation for use by Web Services. In particular, we are concerned with message passing that occurs across organizational boundaries and evaluating the suitability of the Java Messaging Service in this approach.

Keywords: Web Services, Middleware, MOM, Non-repudiation.

1 Introduction

Business communities have traditionally participated in inter-organizational communications via a number of well known techniques such as face-to-face meetings or paper mail. Two important properties associated with inter-organization communications that contribute to successful commerce are reliable information delivery and the trust in the authentication of the originator of the information. Such reliability stems from the ability of a communications medium to provide a level of guarantee for information delivery that is agreed upon by all participants and satisfies the business function as dictated in some contractual agreement. A signature that all parties agree upon as proof of originator is used to provide trust in the origins of information. Inter-organizational disputes are resolved through some legal action directed by appropriate laws. For example, in law the trust mechanism used to overcome a claim of non-repudiation relating to a communication is the witnessing of signature(s).

Electronic commerce makes possible the implementation of existing business practices via enabling digital technologies. Such technologies ease interaction between organizations and the individual by overcoming traditional problems (e.g., paper based, voice) associated to the geographic distribution of participants involved in a business process. The proliferation of the Internet has contributed to the ability of an enterprise to provide their services to a much larger audience than ever envisaged before the existence of widely available public access networks. Furthermore, the properties of electronic communication (e.g., speed, automation) have brought about business processes that would not be possible using non-digital technologies.

M. Malek et al.(Eds.): ISAS 2007, LNCS 4526, pp. 9–19, 2007.
© Springer-Verlag Berlin Heidelberg 2007

To enable the deployment of applications that span organizational boundaries there is a need to enable interactions between organizations in a manner that does not rely on the specific implementation of an organization's technologies yet can promote interoperability in a heterogeneous environment. One possibility for developing such applications is the Object Management Group's CORBA [10] and related specifications. CORBA is a mature specification that provides interoperability for distributed applications built in a heterogeneous environment and is based on the object-oriented paradigm of program development. However, a service based approach using text based messaging as opposed to CORBA's object-oriented approach with binary messaging is considered more suited to inter-organizational application development [11].

Web Services are promoted as providing a suitable paradigm for application integration across organizational boundaries. Services may be implemented and deployed using platform specific mechanisms with interoperability achieved via Web Service standards and communications over standard protocols. The Protocol specified by Web Services is SOAP [7] (providing RPC) with organizations describing their services, and so making them available to clients, via WSDL [12]. WSDL and SOAP are specified using XML [13]. XML allows a developer to represent different elements of data in a text file that may be read and processed by applications (providing appropriate message descriptions for loosely coupled systems).

We propose the use of *message oriented middleware* (MOM) in a solution to satisfying reliable communications while tackling the problem of non-repudiation for Web Services using SOAP and WSDL. We exploit the message passing properties associated with MOM to prevent partial system failure from inhibiting the delivery of messages and prevent limited transient unavailability of clients and servers from resulting in non-completion of a SOAP RPC. Combining persistent messaging with transactional and security mechanisms aids in non-repudiation. Furthermore, our approach maintains message logs to aid in any inter-organizational disputes relating to non-repudiation that may occur. We have implemented our system using only standard technologies, with clients and servers requiring no amendment to use our system. Our system appears transparent to clients and servers.

The main contribution of our paper is to provide the community with an engineered solution that exhibits the benefits of using MOM for non-repudiation and reliability in the context of Web Services. Our purpose was not simply to implement Web Service standards associated to non-repudiation and reliability (on which there are many works).

In the next section we describe our assumptions related to the technologies we use. Section 3 describes our implementation. Section 4 describes related work with section 5 presenting our conclusions and future work.

2   Background

This section gives a short introduction to SOAP and MOM and explains assumptions we make regarding server/client interaction.

2.1   Clients and Servers

We assume clients enact an RPC on a server using SOAP [7] over HTTP across public access networks (i.e., the Internet). This assumption is based on the fact that SOAP over HTTP is the common configuration for accessing Web Services over the Internet [9]. This is due to the expectation that the use of HTTP is widespread and HTTP is conceptually similar to SOAP as they both describe a request/response style protocol (easing the coupling of these protocols). However, the approach of using SOAP over HTTP is not without problems: the best-effort expectations of HTTP to transmit SOAP messages are not appropriate for some applications which require more robust delivery requirements. For example, inter-organizational interactions via SOAP RPC may require non-repudiation properties that provide a basis for determining the validity of messages (as is the subject of this paper).

The use of SOAP is not restricted to client/server interaction that may necessarily result in request/reply style messaging. SOAP messages may be used in a document-literal style that does not depend on a client invoking a particular method on a server and is therefore message based as opposed to RPC based. Furthermore, a SOAP RPC may not necessarily require a server to generate a reply for every request. In this paper we are primarily concerned with SOAP RPC in which every client request results in a server generated reply, even if this reply is simply an acknowledgement of delivery by the server. This decision has been taken as it is assumed clients require an acknowledgement to enable application level decisions to be made on the successfulness of their request. When an RPC crosses organizational boundaries then only via server acknowledgment may a client be able to state a case that it had understood the request to be delivered if a dispute relating to the delivery status of a message arose between client and server.

We assume servers describe their services via WSDL. WSDL provides a means by which servers may describe their services in a manner that allows clients to contact and use such services. Such a description includes the name of the service, the location of the service (typically a URL), methods available for invocation and the input/output parameter types defined for each method.

2.2 Message Passing

As previously described, SOAP RPC over HTTP is the mechanism we assume clients and servers use to interact. However, the best effort reliability of HTTP coupled with lack of non-repudiation techniques requires a different approach to message passing across organizational boundaries. Therefore, we employ message oriented middleware (MOM) as the basis of our approach for inter-organizational message exchange.

MOM allows two or more applications to exchange messages. The CORBA Notification Service [6] and JMS [1] are examples of specifications that describe typical MOM type services. Unlike RPC, there is no requirement for participants in a MOM message exchange to be contactable at the time of communications. In this sense, senders and receivers of messages are decoupled with receivers consuming messages as and when they are able to. This property may be exploited to provide a means of masking client/server unavailability during the enacting of an RPC. For example, a server may be unavailable to service an RPC (e.g., due to high processing loads, administrative downtime). If an RPC is issued by a client during this period a client may get an exception raised that the server may not be able to process the request or the client may timeout the server if the server is unreasonably slow. Either of these scenarios will result in a client managing its own message resends. Consider this example further. Assume a client timeouts a server and reissues a request. Unfortunately, the server actually processed the original request but was simply too slow in returning a response. This results in duplicate request processing, an undesirable problem in distributed applications, but is a considered a more serious problem for inter-organizational communications where such processing may carry a financial penalty for the client. Overcoming this problem requires agreement between clients and servers on unique identification of requests to allow servers to identify repeat requests. However, in relation to non-repudiation this scheme is not easy to implement across organizational boundaries due to the level of trust and the limited degree of information sharing organizations will tolerate.

MOM may employ additional mechanisms to provide reliability guarantees for message exchange. Atomic transactions coupled with persistent messaging provide fault-tolerance in that the failure of the MOM system or any of the participants in message exchange will not necessarily result in the loss of messages. Atomic transactions are used to ensure the underlying persistent store remains consistent and as long as such a store remains correct and reachable then messages will not be lost. Atomic transactions have an all or nothing property in that an attempted amendment to data is either successfully carried out or not carried out at all. Persistence of messages coupled with atomic transactions is desirable in non-repudiation techniques as failure should not render the system incapable of satisfying the requirements of non-repudiation.

3   Implementation

A Java implementation of our system is achieved via Reliable Routing Nodes (RRNs) and the Java Messaging Service (JMS) [1]. The messaging transport used by JMS is HTTP. An RRN receives client requests and server replies and is responsible for attempting to deliver requests/replies to the appropriate servers/clients. Client requests are uniquely identified within the system to enable the tracking of requests and their associated replies. The JMS provides reliable persistent message storage and forwarding for use by an RRN. Client and server interaction is assumed to be modeled in the Web Services domain with messages described via SOAP and services described via WSDL. An RRN is responsible for maintaining a non-repudiation log for recording requests and their associated responses. This log is persistent in nature and is held in a MySQL database.

Our system may be structured as a single RRN or a network of RRNs. In the single RRN approach all clients and servers are serviced by a centralized RRN that is responsible for handling all messages and associated non-repudiation logs. This approach is suited to systems that may exist within a single organizational domain where administration of the RRN system is not shared. When message transmission spans organizational boundaries an approach that uses a network of RRNs is advocated (figure 1). In this approach an RRN may be placed within each organization with inter-organizational communications mirrored by inter-RRN communications. Additional security measures are taken to attempt to ensure messages are genuine and may be trusted. Administration of RRNs is assumed to be shared amongst organizations (responsible for RRNs within their own domains).

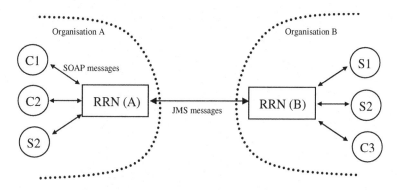

Fig. 1. Network of RRNs facilitating inter-organizational interaction

A non-repudiation log is amended whenever a message is received or sent by an RRN. This log forms the non-repudiation evidence that may be used in inter-organization disputes regarding requests and replies. The use of reliable persistent messaging between organizations together with security measures provides the basis for enabling our approach to non-repudiation. We now describe each component in more detail. For ease of explanation, we shall only consider a single RRN approach in our descriptions unless otherwise stated.

3.1 Providing System Transparency for Clients

The *client handler* is co-located with a client and intercepts client requests before they reach the underlying transport. This requires no changes to the client implementation and the interception of messages is transparent to client operations via the use of handlers as defined in the Axis toolkit [3]. Therefore, we assume the use of the Axis toolkit in client side application development and deployment.

The Axis toolkit eases the development of Web Service based applications by providing a framework for constructing distributed applications that use SOAP for their message exchange (Axis toolkit is commonly described as a SOAP engine). The Axis toolkit includes support for describing Web Services (Web Services Definition Language (WSDL)) and allows a Web Service Deployment Descriptor (WSDD) to be defined that describes the deployment scenario of one or more Web Services. For example, a WSDD may describe the backend components that are used to implement a Web Service. A WSDD may also describe a chain of handlers which SOAP messages pass through during run-time. The ability of a handler to alter messages is exploited by our system to provide RRN transparency to clients.

The client handler intercepts client requests and performs a series of alterations on the message before allowing the message to continue in transit. A new SOAP entry header is created that records the original target endpoint of the request (the Web Service provided by a server). The original target endpoint of the request is replaced by the endpoint that identifies an RRN. This substitution enables the redirection of the request towards the RRN responsible for handling this client's requests. The type of response expected by a client is checked via the identification of return parameters in a message. From such parameters it is possible to determine if a client knows in advance the expected response. This information is inserted into a new header entry and is later used to determine the appropriate tracking of the message.

3.2 Managing Requests and Replies

The *routing provider* (RProvider) is a Web Service that accepts the re-directed requests issued by the client handler. Requests are formatted to an appropriate message structure for handling by the JMS. Client requests are placed in the *request queue* ready to be consumed and processed by the routing server (RServer). In addition to accepting requests directly from the client handler the RProvider is responsible for returning replies to clients. Replies are gained from the *response queue* (JMS). Therefore, the *routing listener* (RLzistener) must derive the appropriately formatted SOAP message from the messages consumed from the response queue before returning a reply to a client. Figure 2 shows the flow of messages throughout the components of an RRN.

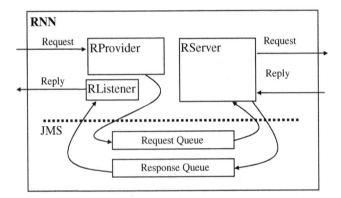

Fig. 2. Components of an RRN

The RServer consumes messages from the request queue and examines the content of each message to determine the appropriate handling of a message. There are two possible actions the RServer may take based on message contents: (i) attempt to issue request to Web Service endpoint as described in a header entry of the message or; (ii) attempt to forward message to another request queue located in another RRN. In (i) the appropriate SOAP message is created from the contents of the JMS message and issued to a Web Service. Replies generated from a request are then formatted to an appropriate message structure for handling by JMS and placed in the response queue. In (ii) the target endpoint described in a message is looked up in a locally held routing table that identifies the RRN the message should be forwarded to. The routing table is XML based and is held locally on the same machine as an RRN. The successful identification of a target RRN results in the RServer (of the originating RRN) attempting to place the message in the target RRN's request queue. The originator node ID (unique across RRNs) is attached to the JMS message as a message property to enable the identification of the originator RRN by the target RRN (required to ensure a reply may be returned to the originator RRN). Ensuring replies are returned to originating

RRNs is the responsibility of the target RRN's RListener. The RListener consumes messages from the response queue that have originator node ID fields set and places such messages on the appropriate originator RRN's response queue (as dictated by the node ID field of the message).

3.3 Undeliverable Messages

Messages that the RServer is unable to deliver to a Web Service (target endpoint) or another RRN's request queue are placed on a *retry queue* (JMS). In the case of an RServer attempting to deliver a message to a Web Service endpoint, messages are identified as undeliverable if exceptions are raised indicating the Web Service is unreachable (either network problems or unavailability of service) or the request timed out. The aborting of the transaction (see 3.4 for more details) within which an RServer was attempting to move a message between request queues indicates an undeliverable message. Periodically messages are moved from the retry queue to the request queue to allow the RServer to attempt message delivery again. The number of retries associated with messages and the frequency with which messages are transferred from the retry queue to the request queue may be set by an administrator of the system. Messages are permanently moved to the failed message queue after the RServer's repeated attempts to deliver the message ended in failure (number of attempts indicated by administrator). When messages are placed on the failed queue information related to why the message failed is appended to the message (e.g., transport exception). The use of retry queues and failed queues by the RServer is mirrored by the response listener in the process of propagating replies back to an originating RRN.

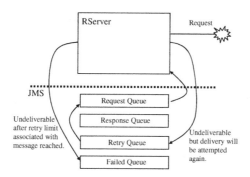

Fig. 3. Handling undeliverable messages

Clients may timeout a request and may not be prepared for a reply when one is available. Furthermore, a client may reissue a request causing duplicate requests to be present in the system. In an attempt to prevent such a scenario the local RRN associates a timeout for each request received. If this timeout expires before a reply is received (consumed by RProvider from *response queue*) a reply is constructed that is in the form of a custom SOAP fault that contains the unique identifier of the related request. This reply is returned to the client. By using this unique identifier in subsequent retries of a request it is possible for clients to retrieve a reply from a request that was previously timed out. This approach does not accommodate client timeouts that expire before an RRN can raise a SOAP fault. However, with clients and an RRN within the same organizational domains we assume it should be possible to tailor the timeout in such a way that clients do not timeout their requests before a SOAP fault may be raised.

3.4 Reliability and Security

Reliable messaging is possible as the JMS specification identifies the ability to ensure guaranteed message delivery even if partial system failure occurs. As described in 3.2, persistent store and delayed message forwarding allow the delivery of messages to endpoints that may suffer transient unavailability (i.e., not able to consume messages as and when messages become deliverable). Furthermore, the persistent nature of the queues ensures that failure of the JMS messaging middleware itself will not lead to the loss of messages (assuming persistent store remains correct and reachable). Our implementation uses the Arjuna Message Service (ArjunaMS) [2], an implementation of the JMS 1.1 specification [1].

Atomic transactions are used whenever message queues are accessed by an RRN. This guarantees that messages are not lost due to RRN failure. If transactions are not available, messages may be lost if an RRN fails after it has consumed a message from one queue before it has placed the same message in another queue.

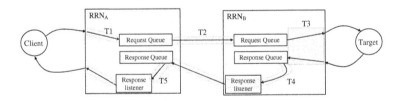

Fig. 4. Transactions satisfying client request

We use the diagram in figure 4 to describe the different transactions involved in satisfying a client request. To improve the clarity of the diagram we have not shown all the components of our system nor have we shown the queues associated with undeliverable messages. When the client issues a request the client handler forwards the client request, say M_1, to the local RRN (RRN$_A$). RRN$_A$ starts a transaction T1 that is successfully completed when M_1 has been placed in the request queue by the RProvider. The process of moving M_1 to the initial target destination (RRN$_B$) is achieved by the RServer and is contained within T2. The RServer takes M_1 from the request queue of RRN$_B$ and issues a request to the target Web Service and waits for a reply. Once a reply, say M_2, is received it is placed in the response queue. However, if M_1 is undeliverable then M_1 is placed in the retry queue. This process is performed within T3. The response listener takes M_2 from the response queue and places M_2 in the response queue of RRN_A within T4. The RListener starts T5 and takes M_2 from the response queue and returns the reply to the client.

In our system we assume that clients and Web Services are non-transactional objects. Therefore, we may assume that the failure of a client or Web Service may result in system inconsistencies. For example, if during T3 a message is successfully delivered to the target Web Service but timeout occurs before a reply is received then M_1 will be placed on the retry queue. However, the target Web Service may be processing M_1 (as it was successfully delivered but the target Web Service was slow returning a reply). RRN_B may reissue M_1 to the target Web Service resulting in an undesirable repeated processing of M_1. If the target Web Service participated as a transactional object within T3 then a timeout (as described previously) may result in an aborted transaction (T3) causing the rollback of the target Web Service state (removing any state changes the delivery of M_1 may have caused) allowing M_1 to be reissued later. This approach may be supported by implementations of WS-Atomic Transaction [4] and WS-Coordination [5] specifications.

As communications may span organizational boundaries we provide security features to ensure that messages sent between RRNs are genuine. A signed digest of the message that is to be sent between RRNs is created and included in the message as a JMS message property. The public key associated to the private key that is used to sign the digest is distributed to all other RRNs. This enables an RRN to verify the identity of the sender of a message: if signing a digest of the message contents with the public key identifies the same set of keys as signing the message with the private key, then the sender is genuine. This precaution provides security in the sense that the identity of a message sender as that of a known RRN. There is a measure of non-repudiation incorporated into such a communication as when an RRN signs a message and it is verified, the administrator of the signing RRN cannot later deny having ever sent the message.

4 Related Work

The work presented in this paper is an engineered solution to non-repudiation and reliability that may be adapted to fit associated Web Service standards. In this section we concentrate on how our system relates to such standards.

A specification exists that enables Web Services to participate in atomic transactions (WS-Atomic Transaction) [4]. As previously mentioned in 3.4, employing atomic transactions for client/server interactions with an RRN would make our system more robust. Furthermore, it may be possible to enhance our system with WS-Atomic Transactions to enable inter-RRN communications. However, allowing clients and servers to interact directly using WS-Atomic Transactions would have the drawback of presenting a tightly coupled environment where transient unavailability of transaction participants would result in the aborting of transactions (a scenario our system attempts to overcome). Furthermore, transactions are a heavyweight process (requiring all participants to carry out two phase commit protocol) and it is unlikely that every RPC would need to be carried out as an atomic transaction. The use of transactions would also inhibit the ability of a client to be released from RPC interaction to continue processing and return at a later time to receive a reply (see 3.3). To implement such a scenario will require more long lived transactions that employ compensation techniques [9], but this approach in itself does not satisfy non-repudiation requirements.

The nature of the implementation of a WS-Transaction service has to be considered in relation to our non-repudiation approach. The coordinator is responsible for determining the outcome of a transaction and is provided by the WS-Coordination service [5]. This makes the coordinator role crucial to the outcome of transactions with the need to ensure all transaction participants trust the coordinator. However, the coordinator must take part in our message logging scheme for non-repudiation to provide similar functionality to our system.

Confluent Software developed its own CORE Web Services Monitoring and Management Platform [8] (which now forms part of Oracle's Identity and SOA Management solutions framework [18]). The purpose of the platform is to allow an organization to implement Service-Oriented Architectures while offering full control over how a service is deployed and executed. Policies that govern how such a service operates may also be described and include Quality of Service, security and message logging. The focus of the CORE platform is on security and logging, although it does provide support for RPC. Our approach is different as we apply a MOM oriented solution.

Work carried out by Maheshwari et al [17] and Tai et al [16] specifically describes a system which enhances Web Service reliability. These works are interesting as MOM is highlighted as a suitable mechanism for implementing underlying reliability for Web Services. Similar observations to our own are made in these papers: loosely coupled MOM architecture is an ideal candidate for underlying messaging infrastructure implementation for Web Services. However, these works do not address the non-repudiation element which we ourselves see as an integral part in any inter-organizational function. However, the reliability element is extensively researched in these papers, with QoS parameters described and testing provided.

5 Conclusions and Future Work

We have developed a system that provides reliable messaging across organizational boundaries while implementing suitable mechanisms for non-repudiation for clients and servers that use SOAP RPC to interact and WSDL to describe services. We have tackled the problem by using a novel approach of employing MOM technologies to achieve inter-organizational communications. By using MOM, the loosely coupled association between sender and receiver has been exploited to prevent limited transient client/server unavailability from hindering successful completion of an RPC. Furthermore, the persistent messaging and transactional services available to MOM technologies ensure that partial failure of our system does not necessarily result in loss of messages.

Our system is built in a modular fashion. We are in the process of tailoring our services so that they adhere more closely to Web Service standards that dictate how non-repudiation and reliability may be utilized.

References

[1] Sun Microsystems, "Java Message Service. Version 1.1, April 12, 2002", http://java.sun.com/products/jms/docs.html as viewed January 2004

[2] D. Ingham, Arjuna Technologies Limited, "ArjunaMS Documentation", http://www.arjuna.com/products/arjunams/index.html as viewed January 2004

[3] Apache Web Services Project, "The Axis Toolkit, version 1.1", http://ws.apache.org/axis/ as viewed January 2004

[4] Arjuna Technologies, Ltd., BEA Systems, Hitachi, Ltd., International Business Machines Corporation, IONA Technologies, Microsoft Corporation, Inc., "Web Services Atomic Transaction (WS-Atomic Transaction)", http://www-128.ibm.com/developerworks/library/specification/ws-tx/, as viewed December 2006

[5] Arjuna Technologies, Ltd., BEA Systems, Hitachi, Ltd., International Business Machines Corporation, IONA Technologies, Microsoft Corporation, "Web Services Coordination (WS-Coordination) Specification", http://www-128.ibm.com/developerworks/library/specification/ws-tx/, as viewed December 2006

[6] OMG, "Notification Service Specification", OMG TC Document telecom/99/07/01, 2000.

[7] The World Wide Web Consortium (W3C), "Simple Object Access Protocol (SOAP) (version 1.1)", W3C Note 08, May 2000

[8] Confluent Software Inc., "Confluent Software Inc Solutions", http://www.confluentsoftware.com/solutions, as viewed September 2003.

[9] K. Gottschalt et al., "Introduction to Web Services Architecture", IBM Systems Journal, Vol 42, No 2, 2002

[10] Object Management Group, "The Common Object Request Broker: Architecture and Specification, 2.3 edition", OMG Technical Committee Document formal/98-12-01, June 1999

[11] A. Gokhale et al., "Reinventing the Wheel? CORBA vs. Web Services", WWW2002, The Eleventh International World Wide Web Conference, Honolulu, Hawaii, USA, 7 – 11 May 2002

[12] The World Wide Web Consortium (W3C), "Web Services Description Language (WSDL) (version 1.1)", W3C Note 15, March 2001

[13] The World Wide Web Consortium (W3C), "Extensible Markup Language (XML) 1.0 (second edition), W3C Recommendation 6 October 2000

[14] Akamai Technologies, Computer Associates International, Inc., Fujitsu Limited, Hewlett-Packard Development Company, International Business Machines Corporation, SAP AG, Sonic Software Corporation, The University of Chicago and Tibco Software Inc., "Web Service Notification (WS Notification) and associated specifications", http://www-128.ibm.com/developerworks/library/specification/ws-notification, as viewed December 2006.

[15] BEA Systems, IBM, Microsoft Corporation, Inc, and TIBCO Software Inc., "Web Services Reliable Messaging Protocol (WS-ReliableMessaging)", http://www-128.ibm.com/developerworks/library/specification/ws-rm/, as viewed December 2006

[16] S. Tai, A. Mikalsen, I. Rouvellou, "Using Message Oriented Middleware for Repiable Web Services", Web Services, E-Business, and the Semantic Web, Springer Berlin / Heidelberg LNCS, Volume 3095/2004, pp 89-104, July 2004

[17] P. Maheshwari, H. Tang, R. Liang, "Enhancing Web Services with Message-Oriented Middleware", Proc. IEEE International Conference on Web Services (ICWS'04), 2004

[18] Oracle Corporation, "Oracle Fusion Middleware", http://www.oracle.com/products/middleware/index.html, as viewed December 2006

Comparing Robustness of AIS-Based Middleware Implementations*

Zoltán Micskei[1], István Majzik[1], and Francis Tam[2]

[1] Dept. of Measurement and Information Systems,
Budapest University of Technology and Economics, Budapest, Hungary
{micskeiz,majzik}@mit.bme.hu
[2] Nokia Research Center, Nokia Corporation, Finlan
francis.tam@nokia.com

Abstract. To enable the interoperability of high availability (HA) middleware systems the Service Availability Forum has released a set of open specifications. The benefit of having open specifications is the choice of implementations available from different vendors. When one chooses a product, one of the selection criteria (besides performance) is the robustness of the implementation, as the crashing or hanging of such a HA middleware causes the failure of the whole system. The challenge is to develop the appropriate technology for measuring and comparing robustness of HA middleware implementations. Based on our earlier results, we present a set of automatic testing tools and a benchmark suite constructed using these tools. We demonstrate the robustness testing approach by comparing the results of benchmarking carried out on three HA middleware implementations.

Keywords: dependability, robustness testing, HA middleware.

1 Introduction

Recently availability became a key factor even in common off-the shelf computing platforms. High availability (HA) can be achieved by introducing manageable redundancy in the system. The common techniques to manage redundancy and achieve minimal system outage can be implemented independently from the application, and can be put on the market as a HA middleware. The standardization of the functionality of such middleware systems has begun as the leading IT companies joined the Service Availability Forum (SA Forum) to elaborate the Application Interface Specification (AIS) [1]. One of the benefits of an open specification is that it enables a company to choose from different vendors, thus reducing the technology risks.

With multiple middleware products developed from the same specification the demand to compare the various implementations naturally arises. The most frequently examined properties are performance and functionality, but especially in case of HA

* The funding of this work by Strategy and Technology, Nokia Networks under the project HASEK in 2006 is acknowledged.

M. Malek et al.(Eds.): ISAS 2007, LNCS 4526, pp. 20–30, 2007.
© Springer-Verlag Berlin Heidelberg 2007

products the dependability is also an important property to be considered. This paper outlines an approach to compare robustness, one of the attributes of dependability of HA middleware systems.

2 Robustness Testing Approach

Robustness is defined as the degree to which a system operates correctly in the presence of *exceptional inputs* or *stressful environmental conditions*. Related work includes API robustness testing and dependability benchmarks. In the Ballista project [2] the robustness of several POSIX implementations were compared using type-specific testing, and several failures were found even in well-known commercial operating systems. Dependability benchmarks aim for a slightly broader goal, to assess the dependability of the complete system. In DBench [3] a conceptual framework was designed and several case studies (e.g. for OS and OLTP systems) were carried out. Based on the above results we elaborated an approach for robustness testing of high availability middleware systems [4]. Because of the complex state-based nature of HA middleware, the previous methods had to be extended.

The first step of developing the test strategy was the identification of the potential *sources* for activating robustness faults in the HA middleware. Figure 1 illustrates these sources, considering a typical computing node of a HA distributed system, as follows:

1. External errors: They affect the operation of the application, thus their effects reach the HA middleware only indirectly (through normal, erroneous or missing API calls).
2. Operator errors: In general, operator errors appear as erroneous configuration of the middleware and erroneous calls using the specific management interface.
3. API calls: The calls of the application components using the public interfaces of the HA middleware can lead to failures if they use exceptional values, e.g. NULL pointer or improperly initialized structures.
4. OS calls: The robustness of a system is also characterized by its ability to handle the exceptions or error codes returned by the OS services it uses.
5. Hardware failures: The most significant HW failures in a HA system are host and communication failures (that has to be tolerated in the normal operating mode of the HA middleware) and lack of system resources.

From the above sources the following ones were selected to be included in the first version of the dependability benchmark suite:

- The standardized middleware API calls are considered as a potential source of activating robustness faults. Because of the high number of possible exceptional value combinations and scenarios, the elements of the robustness tests suite were automatically generated by tools. The challenge in testing the API calls was that most of the AIS interface functions are state-based, i.e. a proper initialization call sequence, middleware configuration and test arrangement is required, otherwise a trivial error code is returned.

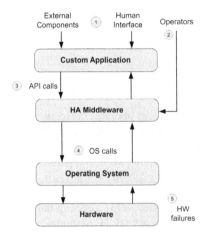
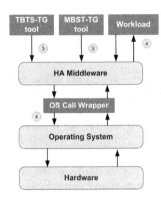

Fig. 1. HA middleware fault model   **Fig. 2.** Testbed tools

- The failures of the OS system calls were included for the following reason. They do not only represent the faults of the OS itself (which has lower probability for mature operating systems), but failures in other software components, in the underlying hardware and in the environment also could manifest in an error code returned by a system call. Possible examples of such conditions are writing data to a full disk, communication errors when sending a message, etc.
- Studies show that operator errors cause also a significant part of service unavailability, however, the configuration of the HA middleware and the system management interface are still under standardization by the SA Forum, thus they were not included in the current version of the benchmark suite.

3 Testbed Tools and Benchmark Suite

Taking into consideration the potential sources of activating robustness faults, a set of tools was developed to assist the activation of these faults by generating proper test values and performing the test calls. This dependability benchmark testbed is depicted in Figure 2. In the following, we describe these tools and the benchmark suite developed for testing version B.02.01 of the AIS Availability Management Framework (AMF). Although the API of the AMF is standardized, the implementations selected for testing (two versions of openais [5] and one version of SAFE4TRY [6], see Section 4) influenced the realization of the test execution environment.

3.1 Template-Based Type-Specific Test Generator

The template-based type-specific test generator (TBTS-TG) uses the following approach to generate robustness test cases that realize calls to the HA middleware API with exceptional values. Instead of defining the exceptional cases one by one for each API function, the exceptional values are defined with regard to the parameter *types* that are used in the functions. From the description of these types, the tool generates a *test program* for each API function, and this test program calls the given function with all combinations of the specified values. Each combination is executed in a new process to separate the test cases from each other, and the result code of the call is logged after completion. The test case is considered to detect a robustness failure if the test program or the middleware implementation crashes or hangs (e.g. due to a segmentation fault or a timeout). To help diagnosing the robustness faults, the first calls contain only a single exceptional value (using valid values in the case of the remaining parameters).

The inputs and outputs of the tool are presented in Figure 3. The skeleton of the test program is prepared manually as an XSL template. The metadata of the functions and types to test are specified in XML files. The exceptional and valid values are defined as C code snippets. For simple types, e.g. numbers and enumerations, values recommended by traditional testing techniques were selected, like valid values, boundary values and values outside the domain of the given type. In the case of complex structures the following systematic method was used: for each member there are test cases that assign invalid values to the given member while the other members remain valid.

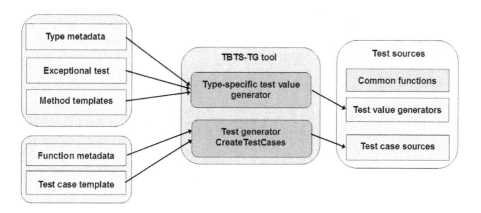

Fig. 3. Architecture of TBTS-TG tool

The first version of the benchmark suite consisted of standalone C programs that called the AIS API functions directly (outside of the AMF). In the current version the AMF service of the middleware starts the test programs configured as SA-aware components. To support the automatic execution of the benchmark suite a *test execution engine* was prepared. This engine runs the same test programs on each HA middleware, only the following tasks are implementation-dependent (as these are not standardized by the SA Forum): (i) construction of an implementation-specific configuration file on the basis of a common abstract configuration (which consists of one service group and one service unit containing the actual test case as a single component), and (ii) restarting the middleware between the runs of the test cases.

3.2 Mutation-Based Sequential Test Generator

While the TBTS-TG tool tests mostly individual functions, the mutation-based sequential test generator (MBST-TG) could be used to generate complex call sequences. The basic idea of the tool is that *mutation operators* representing typical robustness faults, like omitting a call or changing the specified order of calls, are applied to valid functional test programs that use the HA middleware. In this way a large number of complex robustness test cases can be obtained automatically.

The challenge of implementing the MBST-TG tool was the parsing and modification of the test programs' C source files. As the available free parsers encountered various problems when system header files were included in the input files, we followed a light-weight approach instead of obtaining the full parse tree (that is required for compilation). The srcML tool [7] was used to build an XML file representing only the *syntactic structure* of the input source files. This syntactic structure is enough to implement the common mutation operators.

Currently five mutation operators are implemented: omission, relocation and swapping of calls, modifying conditions, replacing parameters. The inputs of the MBST-TG (Figure 4) are the source files to be mutated and a configuration file that describes the parameterization of the mutation operator, e.g. the filters to be used when searching for a call to apply the mutation. Note that occasionally the mutation may result in such source code that cannot be compiled (data flow analysis is not performed, this way, for example, changing of function calls may result in using variables that were not assigned a value before).

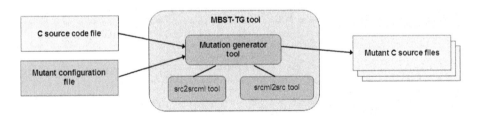

Fig. 4. Architecture of the MBST-TG tool

The mutant candidates came from two sources. The first one was the SAF Test [8] project, which is an open-source conformance test suite for SA Forum specifications. Because the test cases in SAF Test are redundant, 10 source files could be selected that cover the functionality of the others as well. The source files had to be slightly modified, because the current SAF Test does not use the required LDAP Distinguished Name (DN) format for component names. The second source was the functional test suite provided in openais, from which the testamf test file was used for mutation. The MBST-TG tool was configured to generate (i) two mutants using each operator in the case of each input file (using one operator each time) and (ii) ten mutants in case of each input file using two random operators each time. Altogether from these mutants 92 valid mutants were included in the test suite.

3.3 OS Call Wrapper Tool

The OS call wrapper intercepts system calls executed by the HA middleware and injects exceptional values into their return values (Figure 5). Since the middleware is tested here as a black box, the system calls can be triggered only indirectly, by starting a workload application.

The OS call wrapper can be configured to *intercept* or *delay* selected system calls. The return value of an intercepted call could be (i) the actual value returned by the original system call, if the call was also forwarded to the OS, (ii) a predefined valid or exceptional value or (iii) a randomly selected value from the possible error codes of the function. The wrapper is implemented using the Unix LD_PRELOAD variable, which can be used to load predefined libraries instead of system libraries.

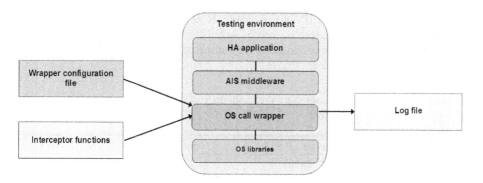

Fig. 5. Architecture of the OS call wrapper based testing

As a *workload* to trigger OS calls from the middleware, a synthetic HA application was prepared that resembles a search and index engine. The application utilizes the AMF and checkpoint service of the middleware. Using the *strace* utility all system calls of the middleware were logged during the execution of the workload application on both openais and SAFE4TRY, and the intersection of the two sets of OS calls was included in the benchmark suite, namely the functions accept, bind, close, gettimeofday, munmap, poll, sendmsg, setsockopt and socket.

4   Robustness Testing Results

The benchmark suite created by the above tools was used to test the robustness of the following implementations: (1) the *SAFE4TRY* evaluation package from Fujitsu Siemens Computers, which consists of the SAF AIS implementation RTP-SAF-L V2.1A and the PRIMECLUSTER cluster foundation, and (2) *openais*, an open source implementation of the AIS specification, including its version 0.80.1 (the latest stable release) and the trunk (the latest development version directly from the source control system of the project).

4.1   Results from the Type-Specific Tests

Just by trying to compile the test suite on the system under test, several discrepancies were found: The header files used in openais differ in eight places from the official header files of the AIS specification, and thus from the header files used by the test suite. There is also one misspelling in SAFE4TRY's header files. Moreover, there are several types in the specification that are mapped to different types in the implementations, e.g. SaInt32T is mapped to *long* in SAFE4TRY and to *int* in openais.

Table 1 summarizes the exit codes of the test cases that were logged when executing the benchmark suite. Segmentation faults definitely indicate robustness failures, since in a HA middleware even invalid inputs should be handled correctly. Timeouts could indicate normal behavior, because some of the API functions could be parameterized to wait for an event to dispatch. However, while examining the concrete values used in the benchmark it turned out that the large number of timeouts in openais-trunk and openais-0.80.1 is not reasonable. Note for openais-0.80.1 there are less calls listed in the table because in case of saAmfProtectionGroupTrack the test program and the middleware crashed at the beginning of the test and no calls were executed for that functions.

Table 1. The number of test cases that exited with the given status code in case of type-specific testing of the different platforms

Status code	openais-0.80.1	openais-trunk	SAFE4TRY
0 (success)	24568	26019	29663
11 (seg. fault)	1110	1468	0
14 (timeout)	467	2178	2

Segmentation faults occurred in 13 functions of openais-trunk and in 12 functions of openais-0.80.1. Timeouts were observed in 7 functions of openais-trunk, in 7 different functions of openais-0.80.1, and in one function of SAFE4TRY (namely, in saAmfDispatch when specifying a flag representing blocking; here timeout is the correct behavior). For the details, see Table 2.

Some of the test cases caused fatal error in the middleware. The tests for 14 functions in openais-0.80.1 and for 6 functions in openais-trunk produced an internal *assertion violation* and the middleware exited. The following two assertion violations were observed:

```
aisexec: amf_lib_exit_fn: Assertion `comp != ((void *)0)' failed.
aisexec: amfcomp.c:1142: amf_comp_register: Assertion `0' failed.
```

In the case of SAFE4TRY, after executing the test program for saAmfProtection-GroupTrackStop() the stopping of the middleware was not successful.

Table 3 details the different error codes for the successful calls. Every AMF call has a handle parameter, which is checked first before any operation. All tested AIS implementations could process the incorrectly initialized handles well, as it can be seen from the high number of SA_AIS_ERR_BAD_HANDLE codes. The number of SA_AIS_ERR_INVALID_PARAM codes show that SAFE4TRY detects much more invalid parameter combinations. When an assertion was violated in openais, all the remaining calls for the given test program resulted in library error, that is the reason of the high number of SA_AIS_ERR_LIBRARY codes. In the case of SAFE4TRY, library errors were observed for the saAmfHealthcheckConfirm and saAmfHealth-checkStop functions. In both versions of openais a significant number of test cases returned invalid error codes, which cannot be considered as a robust behavior.

Table 2. Functions that produced robustness failures in case of type-specific testing

Failure	openais-0.80.1	openais-trunk
seg. fault	saAmfComponentErrorClear, saAmfComponentErrorReport saAmfComponentNameGet, saAmfComponentRegister, saAmfComponentUnregister, saAmfHAStateGet, saAmfHealthcheckConfirm, saAmfHealthcheckStart, saAmfHealthcheckStop, saAmfInitialize, saAmfProtectionGroupTrackStop, saAmfSelectionObjectGet	saAmfComponentErrorClear, saAmfComponentErrorReport saAmfComponentNameGet, saAmfComponentRegister, saAmfComponentUnregister, saAmfHAStateGet, saAmfHealthcheckConfirm, saAmfHealthcheckStart, saAmfHealthcheckStop, saAmfInitialize, saAmfProtectionGroupTrack, saAmfProtectionGroupTrackStop, saAmfSelectionObjectGet
timeout	saAmfComponentErrorClear, saAmfComponentNameGet, saAmfCSIQuiescingComplete, saAmfDispatch, saAmfInitialize, saAmfHealthcheckConfirm, saAmfProtectionGroupTrackStop	saAmfComponentErrorClear, saAmfComponentNameGet, saAmfComponentUnregister, saAmfCSIQuiescingComplete, saAmfDispatch, saAmfProtectionGroupTrack, saAmfProtectionGroupTrackStop

Table 3. The number of test cases that finished and returned the given SaAisErrorT error code in case of type-specific testing of the different platforms

Error code	openais-0.80.1	openais-trunk	SAFE4TRY
SA_AIS_ERR_BAD_FLAGS	0	0	384
SA_AIS_ERR_BAD_HANDLE	18828	20408	20708
SA_AIS_ERR_EXIST	0	0	1
SA_AIS_ERR_INIT	0	0	6
SA_AIS_ERR_INVALID_PARAM	56	226	6073
SA_AIS_ERR_LIBRARY	3953	2316	52
SA_AIS_ERR_NOT_EXIST	0	1296	1786
SA_AIS_ERR_NOT_SUPPORTED	0	0	144
SA_AIS_ERR_TRY_AGAIN	30	30	0
SA_AIS_ERR_VERSION	336	336	294
SA_AIS_OK	86	128	215
invalid error code	1279	1279	0

In our previous work [4] version 0.69 of openais (based on version A.01.01 of the AMF specification) was used for benchmarking. In comparison with these previous experiments, the following could be observed: the simple method of using only invalid pointers and integer values as exceptional parameters did not activate so many robustness failures in the current versions of openais. One of the reasons for this is that moving to version B.01.01 of AMF the number of pointer parameters decreased significantly. 58.6% of the tests in the type-specific robustness test suite resulted in segmentation fault for version 0.69, while this number was only 4.2% and 4.9% for the 0.80.1 and trunk versions, respectively. Thus, the robustness of openais was definitely improved, although it still lags behind the robustness of SAFE4TRY, where the only robustness problem discovered by the benchmark suite was the error code SA_AIS_ERR_LIBRARY for two functions.

4.2   Results from the Mutation-Based Testing

The mutant test sequences obtained from SAF Test and testamf were executed on the three implementations. The number of observed robustness failures is summarized in Table 4.

Table 4. The number of observed robustness failures / the total number of executed test cases in case of mutation-based testing of the different platforms

Input	openais-0.80.1	openais-trunk	SAFE4TRY
SAF Test	8 / 63	0 / 63	1 / 63
testamf	22 / 29	28 / 29	0 / 29

The robustness failures discovered by the SAF Test mutants were the following. In case of eight mutants, openais-0.80.1 exited with one of the previous or with the following assertion:

```
./aisexec: symbol lookup error: /opt/openais-
0.80.1/exec//service_amf.lcrso: undefined symbol: assert
```

In SAFE4TRY, when stopping the middleware after one of tests the following error occurred:

```
Error in communication! ERROR: Stopping AMF subsystem was not
successful
```

Note that the SAF Test programs are constructed in such a way that the return value is checked after each function call, and if it does not match the predefined value then the program is aborted with an error message. This feature of the SAF Test programs makes them difficult to be used in robustness tests, because the subsequent calls are not executed if a wrong return value is detected.

When the testamf mutants were executed as AMF components in openais-trunk and openais-0.80.1 the CPU utilization increased to 100% and a hard reset had to be performed. Thus, Table 4 contains the results from running the testamf mutants as standalone programs. During the experiments with the mutants the above detailed assertions were also observed.

It could be observed that mutation based robustness testing highlighted additional robustness failures that were not detected by the type-specific tests. It gives reasons for applying such complex test sequences.

4.3 Results from the OS Wrapper

For each of the 9 system calls (see Section 3.3) a separate test case was executed by starting the workload application and after a while forcing a failover. During the execution the system calls were forwarded to the OS, and with a predefined probability a random error code was returned (the probability depended on the frequency of the call, which was determined in probe runs).

Table 5. The system calls that provided the given outcome using the OS call wrapper

Outcome	openais-0.80.1	openais-trunk	SAFE4TRY
No failure observed	accept, close, gettimeofday, munmap, sendmsg, setsockopt	accept, bind, close, gettimeofday, sendmsg	accept, close, gettimeofday, sendmsg, setsockopt
Application failed	-	munmap, setsockopt	poll
Middleware failed	bind, poll, socket	poll, socket	bind, munmap, socket

The first row of Table 5 lists the system calls in which case the workload application was executed successfully in spite of the injected fault. The second row shows such cases when the application exited but the middleware did not fail. The last row indicates the test cases when also the middleware exited (typically silently, without error messages). Note that due to the random injection of error codes, these latter cases just indicate potential robustness faults without objectively comparing the implementations.

5 Conclusion

In this paper a robustness testing approach for HA middleware systems was presented. The novelty of the approach is the application of *automatic tools* that construct the test cases systematically on the basis of the *standard interface specification* (API functions) and existing functional test suites. The robustness testing of the HA middleware implementations demonstrated that these tools can be used efficiently and their test results are complementary as they detect distinct failure types. It turned out that there are still *several robustness problems* both in version 0.80.1 and in the trunk version of the openais implementation. SAFE4TRY turned out to be much more robust with regard to the exceptional inputs generated by the benchmark suite. It is important to emphasize, however, that robustness testing was used only to observe these problems, and further work is needed to find the causes and to turn the observations into dependability benefits, e.g. by identifying the wrong implementation approaches or coding errors that shall be corrected. The work with AIS-based implementations will be continued in the HIDENETS project (IST 26979) which develops resilience solutions for distributed applications.

References

1. Service Availability Forum, Application Interface Specification, February 2006., URL: http://www.saforum.org/
2. P. Koopman *et al.*, "Automated Robustness Testing of Off-the-Shelf Software Components," in *Proceedings of Fault Tolerant Computing Symposium*, pp. 230-239, Munich, Germany, June 23-25, 1998.
3. K. Kanoun *et al.*, "Benchmarking Operating System Dependability: Windows 2000 as a Case Study," in *Proceedings of 10th Pacific Rim International Symposium on Dependable Computing*, Papeete, French Polynesia, 2004.
4. Z. Micskei, I. Majzik and F. Tam, "Robustness Testing Techniques For High Availability Middleware Solutions," in *Proc. of Int. Workshop on Engineering of Fault Tolerant Systems (EFTS 2006)*, Luxembourg, Luxembourg, 2006.
5. OpenAIS, AIS implementation, URL: http://developer.osdl.org/dev/openais/
6. Fujitsu Siemens Computers, SAFE4 Continuous Services, SAFE4TRY version, URL: http://www.safe4cs.com
7. Software Development Laboratory, srcML, URL: http://www.sdml.info/projects/srcml/
8. SAF Test, SAF-conformance test suite, URL: http://saftest.sourceforge.net/

Service-Oriented Operating System: A Key Element in Improving Service Availability

Nikola Milanovic[1] and Miroslaw Malek[2]

[1] Berlin University of Technology
nmilanov@cs.tu-berlin.de
[2] Humboldt University Berlin
malek@informatik.hu-berlin.de

Abstract. The operating system's role is often neglected in the availability analysis of modern, service-oriented applications. The usual argumentation is that the underlying OS seems to be irrelevant in the world of today's web-centric applications. We propose a framework for construction of "service-oriented operating system" and examine the role it plays in physical and user-perceived service availability by investigating potential abstractions and integration points between service-oriented applications and OS architecture, such as treating OS as a set of collaborating services, introducing standard middleware services as parts of an OS and including support for server consolidation through virtualization. We demonstrate how to address the following dependability attributes at the OS level: service availability (readiness for correct service), service reliability (continuity of correct service), integrity (absence of improper system alterations) and maintainability (ability to undergo modifications and repair). We further argue that availability at the OS level plays the key role in the availability of service-oriented applications and propose an orthogonal OS design methodology suited for that purpose.

1 Introduction

The term service-oriented architecture (SOA) emerged in [1] to describe the approach of building loosely coupled distributed systems with minimal shared understanding among system components. Sometimes the term service-oriented computing (SOC) is used instead to describe the computing paradigm that uses SOA. The main building blocks in SOA are services. Services are self-describing, open components that support rapid, low-cost development and deployment of distributed applications. The main goal of SOA is transparent, flexible and dynamic interaction of services and their clients over multiple interconnected domains. The benefits of SOA include increased efficiency through task outsourcing and component reuse, easier integration, increased flexibility and agility at business and IT level, development of composite applications, enabling of multi-vendor application sourcing, and on-demand interconnection with business partners. SOA can be deployed at different levels of granularity: from exposing fine-grained technical functions to coarse-grained business or scientific operations and processes. SOA is based on the model of roles: service providers publish

M. Malek et al.(Eds.): ISAS 2007, LNCS 4526, pp. 31 – 42, 2007.
© Springer-Verlag Berlin Heidelberg 2007

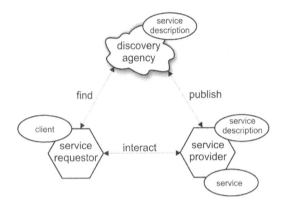

Fig. 1. Roles and interactions in SOA

machine-readable description of their capabilities to directories, and clients browse directories to find adequate operations. This model is sometimes called publish-find-interact (Figure 1).

The de-facto standard for SOA implementation today is the Web Service Architecture (WSA). It defines SOA as a distributed system in which agents, also known as services, coordinate by message passing [7]. SOA is characterized by the following properties: logical view of the system, message orientation, description orientation, fine granularity, and platform neutrality. Web services are, however, not the only way to realize an SOA.

From the development perspective, SOA is not a revolution but rather, from a historical viewpoint, an evolution. It is traditionally claimed that SOA has its roots in the fields of programming languages, distributed systems and business computing (Figure 2) [8]. Conspicuously absent from this figure are operating systems. Modern operating systems are general purpose systems, although some server operating systems introduce slight optimizations towards server applications (e.g., modified scheduling quantum or implicit multiprocessor support). The role of a general purpose OS is to control resources and provide a base API for the application programs to be written [13]. Therefore, the role is twofold: providing extended (virtual) machine and resource management (time- and space-multiplexing). Most operating systems abstractions (e.g., threads of virtual memory) were not designed explicitly for server or dynamic service-based environments. The modern application landscape has evolved into a heterogeneous, distributed and dynamic processes model, where actors are separated by technological, business and legal barriers. The explosive growth in the development of middleware technologies aiming to support and connect different aspects of the new process model emphasises the operating system inadequacy further. In this paper, it is argued that extension of basic OS concepts to suit the special properties of service-oriented systems such as dependability can be essential to increase service availability.

The remainder of the paper is structured as follows: we first investigate general properties of service-oriented systems (Section 2.1) and try to establish possible levels of abstraction and integration between SOC and OS concepts (Section 2.2). In Section 2.3 we describe properties, such as support for client-server interaction, dependability, prediction, and evolution that can be achieved by structuring an OS according to SOC principles. Finally, Section 2.4 examines available OS architectures and proposes a novel orthogonal design methodology. Section 3 concludes with a discussion on availability enhancements that new OS-level abstractions introduce.

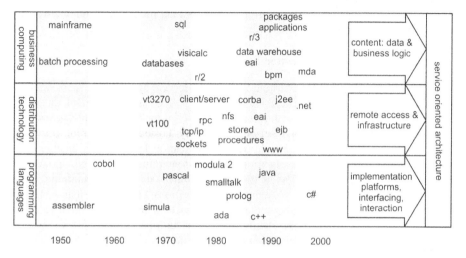

Fig. 2. SOC history

2 Goals

Due to heterogeneous and distributed nature of SOC applications, it is very difficult to apply classical dependability and availability methodologies to achieve and improve availability of already deployed SOC applications. The reasons are different application containers, legal issues, barriers, access rights, and technologies used in the integration of component based applications into services. For example, checkpointing or parsing log files are not trivial operations in complex applications spanning multiple domains administered by different authorities. Therefore, addressing availability at the OS level seems to be a reasonable approach to conquer complexity of the SOC landscape. Having dependability primitives and principles addressed at the OS level enables unification of dependability properties at the application level. Up to date, surprisingly little attention has been paid to supporting principles of SOC (and especially availability) at the OS layer. Some notable exceptions like [15] do not represent common or systematic trend.

What is a service-oriented operating system? Is it an operating system structured and built on the principles of service-oriented computing? Or is it an operating system that is tailored to suit special properties of service-oriented systems? Is it a single-processor, multi-processor, network or distributed OS? Is it all of the above, or none of the above? Is there a need for service-oriented operating system? What is wrong with the existing OS designs and implementations? Do we need a fundamentally different role(s) apart from memory/process and file management? Should we clearly address dependability at this level? We will start answering these questions by investigating distinguishing properties of service-oriented systems and examining the possible levels of abstraction and integration between the SOC, OS concepts and dependability.

We focus on the following dependability attributes, as defined in [16]: service availability (readiness for correct service), service reliability (continuity of correct service), integrity (absence of improper system alterations) and maintainability (ability to undergo modifications and repair).

2.1 Properties of Service-Oriented Systems

The main difference between traditional client-server applications and service-oriented applications is that instead of monolithic server application and fat client, thin clients are communicating with relatively coarse-grained server applications built dynamically out of fine-grained services, possibly hosted by different providers and/or organizations. Furthermore, the entire application landscape is changed and enriched: there are multiple application servers containing distributed application business logic and service implementations, (distributed) databases containing application data and multiple clients executing compositions of services that were not predicted and predefined at deployment time. Services also offer machine readable description (metadata) and can be ideally selected at runtime. Let us try to summarize distinctive characteristics of a service-oriented system:

- application components (services) offer metadata of various expressiveness (functional and non-functional properties)
- applications are constructed by service (component) composition using variety of methods and tools
- efficient service discovery procedure is the key to locating adequate composition partners
- service level agreements (SLA) or contracts are used to describe conditions between service consumer (client) and service provider
- applications are inherently distributed and loosely coupled: application dependability and security are complex functions of availability/security of remote services, their application containers and the network
- since services are provided within separate technological, business and legal domains, trust is essential
- due to distributed and loosely-coupled nature of applications, mechanisms for reliable messaging and consensus (transactions) are required

The fact is that the properties listed here concerning the structure, design, implementation and runtime of service-based systems are most of the time ignored at the OS level.

2.2 Possible Levels of Abstraction and Integration

It is possible to identify several levels at which OS and SOC can be abstracted and integrated:

- OS as a set of collaborating services
- Middleware services as OS services

- Server consolidation through virtualization
- Application container services

In the remainder of this section, each level will be investigated in turn.

OS as a set of collaborating services. This is the way to create an OS based on service-oriented principles. All OS kernel calls are exposed as services offering machine readable description in terms of properties such as time, resource usage, security or dependability. Such OS has a layered structure shown in Figure 3. At the bottom layer basic kernel services are constructed, described and published. At the composition layer, kernel services interact (are composed) and the correctness of the composition is optionally proved. Finally, at the top layer services are managed in terms of trust, certification, liability or dependability. What is the advantage of architecting such an OS? Besides natural mapping from the application layer to the OS layer, the possibility of creating "safe" OS through verification and "reliable" OS through automatic failover are some exciting possibilities. In essence, OS calls are dynamically constructed out of available kernel services which communicate using interprocess communication (IPC) mechanism. Adding contracts to kernel services enables formal and run-time verification. When some of them are unavailable, automatic failover/substitution can be performed transparently thus increasing OS robustness.

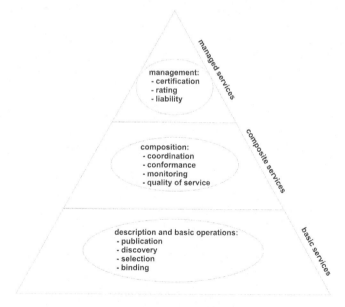

Fig. 3. Layered view of OS services

Middleware services as OS services. Current service-oriented applications are enabled with middleware technologies such as message oriented middleware (MOM) [9] or enterprise service bus (ESB) [2]. The main role of the middleware is to support specific properties of SOA applications, such as discovery, message routing or security. Typical ESB architecture is shown in Figure 4.

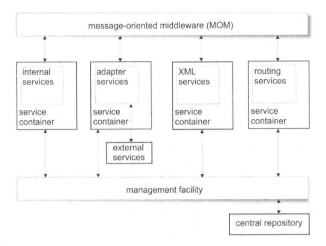

Fig. 4. Enterprise service bus

ESB constructs SOA by integrating "accidental architectures" into a decentralized infrastructure called service bus, which is inherently message-based, asynchronous and loosely coupled. In ESB all applications are provided as (business) services and connected via reliable, secure and managed virtual channels. The main consequence is that orchestration, transformation and maintenance can be moved to the bus and processed in a controlled manner. The main elements of ESB are: message oriented middleware (MOM), service containers, management facility, routing and XML-processing. Arguably, the most important element is MOM. The task of MOM is to support reliable and asynchronous message exchange. In ESB architecture, all direct (or legacy) communication channels are replaced by virtual channels, managed by MOM. That way, strongly coupled, synchronous, point-to-point interactions (method invocations) are replaced by loosely coupled indirect interaction implemented using message passing.

ESB can be understood as an application container for service-based applications. When considering service oriented OS, it would seem natural to move some elements of the middleware to the OS level. Hence, methods for message passing between services could be integrated into IPC mechanism, and support for routing (itinerary based, orchestration and content based) and XML processing (discovery and communication) could be added to the kernel of the potential OS that should support ESB on top of it. Parallels between reliability at the kernel level and service (application) level should be established (e.g., making support for WS-Policy at the application level easier by facilitating it with adequate primitives in the kernel IPC mechanism).

Server consolidation through virtualization. Another aspect of service-oriented applications is the trend of server consolidation. With the cost of space, electricity and maintenance being prevalent compared to the hardware cost, more and more companies are trying to reduce the costs by migrating multiple applications (with all accompanying infrastructure) to single servers by the means of virtualization. Different kinds of virtualization will be detailed in the Section 2.4, but the basic idea is to provide OS virtualization support, as well as to investigate the overall usefulness of virtualization in the given context. It has already been argued that virtualization is not suited for (internet) server systems [14]. The argument is that OS should eliminate the abstraction of resource virtualization with the ultimate goal of enabling fine-grained resource control.

Application container services. The majority of modern SOA applications are developed by integrating existing applications realized using component-based technologies (e.g., J2EE or .NET). The essential elements of such applications are application servers (containers). In the context of SOC, application servers are entities that host remote services. Application servers provide services with infrastructural capabilities such as transaction processing, logging and security. One of the major problems of SOC is the need to integrate divergent and incompatible application server support mechanisms. For example, if two components exposed as services should cooperate in solving a complex task, it may be necessary to execute the composition within a single transaction, which may require integration of different transaction management mechanisms. This is neither trivial nor always possible. Therefore, additional support at the OS level can be introduced that will facilitate application server services' interaction, simulation and cooperation.

2.3 Properties Achieved with Service-Oriented OS

Assuming that one (or more) level from the previous section is selected as feasible, let us examine with which properties and through what means a "dependable service-oriented aware OS" can be developed.

Support for client-service interaction. An SOA system can be represented at the OS level as a set of processes with assigned resource constraints, such as memory capacity or processor time. Process may or may not correspond one-to-one to external or internal (kernel) services. Because meta-information (service description) is available, OS design can be optimized. Service or process composition can be constructed as graphs that can be mapped into OS concepts such as process groups, jobs or task sets. Considering service contracts (service level agreements), scheduling can be optimized such that contracts are adequately fulfilled. Modern server running any available OS can be seen as a stream processor. Two basic strategies for request processing are distinguished: threaded and event-driven processing. They, however, do not take into account the complex distributed and threaded structure of SOA applications where multiple threads (usually distributed across server boundaries) represent actors such as application server(s), service implementations, databases, etc. The issue with threaded scheduling is that only coarse-grained resource control is possible. Furthermore, blocking I/O limits concurrency, hence the issue of reliable asynchronous coordination between the actors using IPC requires us to revisit properties of time- and space-decoupling, similarly to the context of LINDA coordination language [4]. The issue of efficient service discovery must also be supported at the OS level, either through directory or matchmaking mechanisms.

Dependability. Fault isolation is of the paramount importance in the OS design [12]. Using contracts can make sandboxing easier thus improving OS reliability. Even in the case where kernel function (service) disobeys its contract, a substitution can be located and recomposed into the request transparently. The issue of automatic failover at the OS level highlights two important issues: support for failover at the application level by introducing adequate mechanisms at the OS level and the concept of the OS as a set of *partially redundant* or *overlapping* kernel services. Revisiting Figure 3, a mechanism for fault tolerance at the composition layer can be introduced by recomposition of services from the bottom layer. Principally that would mean that kernel calls could be constructed dynamically and on-demand. This is similar to the N-version programming paradigm [10]. Translated to the OS level that would mean that several versions of the same service (process) are started simultaneously in order to improve both performance and availability (increase chances of successful task completion). The challenge here is to invoke functionally equivalent services and vote on them in such a way that either consensus or majority outcome is considered as a correct result of a requested service. For performance improvement the fastest response to a request for a service would be taken. An alternative would be a recovery-block scheme [11] which seems to be highly suitable for service-oriented infrastructure where upon failure, functionally equivalent service would be automatically invoked. In a simplified homogeneous multiple service environment several space and time redundancy schemes have been reviewed and evaluated in [3].

As SOC is based on client-service interaction, load-balancing should be introduced at the OS layer by modifying scheduler to support relief techniques such as load decrease or call rejection. This is supported by contracts and service level agreements. Especially in the case of distributed OS, state clean up (rejuvenation, garbage collection, elimination of useless processing) can improve scheduling performance. Rejuvenation techniques such as reboot, restart, and reset of one or more services (processes) improve availability. Transactions and checkpoints are fundamental elements, but as far as SOC is concerned, a distributed transaction mechanism may not be the optimal one as it may lead to potentially long term resource locking. Split (open nested) transaction model may be more appropriate, where one big transaction (comprising many processes) is split into a number of smaller transactions (which can but must not correspond to single services or processes) and each of the sub-transactions may commit independently, without waiting for others. However, the drawback is that in case of rollback, compensation actions must be provided up front, which is not always possible. Potentially interesting issue may be the realization of exception handling mechanism at the composite or managed services layer, see Figure 3, as a means of forward error correction.

Prediction. We set this property apart, although it is a part of dependability. The main reason is that available methods for modelling of complex software systems simply do not scale well for industrial complexity levels. Not only complexity is an issue but also frequent dynamic configuration change, updates and upgrades. Therefore, OS should be *instrumented* in order to enable efficient variable selection and tracking. Selected variables describing the system current state are used as input to various failure prediction models which can be data or event driven. Instrumentation can be performed at the low service level (basic services from Figure 3) and prediction is then performed at the middle and topmost level, depending on the criteria. The simplest examples are resource or failure predictions [5], [6].

Self-* properties. Closely related to dependability and prediction is the spectrum of self-* properties, such as self-diagnosis, self-healing, self-repair, self-management or self-configuration. They all imply certain degree of automation of the otherwise costly processes. Self-* properties can be realized at the upper layer of the hierarchy shown in Figure 3, within the framework of managed services. Thus both basic and composite services become enabled with self-* properties. For example, self-configuration can be performed through SLA enforcement and self-healing through automatic failover (substitution) or recomposition.

Security. One of the critical properties is the OS security and its resilience to attacks, viruses and any attempts to derail the system. The challenge is magnified as the service environments are normally widely distributed. Security at the OS level is addressed at the architecture level (e.g., using microkernel solution), or at the service level (verification of correctness and creating "safe" OS).

Trust. It is unrealistic to expect that all important properties within an OS can be formally verified in design and/or at runtime. Therefore, an elaborate trust mechanism has to be introduced, to support correctness at the application level as well as to enforce internal OS consistency. There are several available forms of trust management, but the most frequent one is a reputation system. By tracking and logging behavior of kernel services, reputation tables can be set up and contract validation can be performed. It can lead to dynamic selection of optimal kernel and external services at runtime, and to discovery of bugs or bad design. The trivial example would be to keep track of declared performance and usage of server resources. Given enough time, optimal scheduling and memory management policies for different tasks would be profiled that way.

Migration and evolution. One of the main requirements of SOA applications is platform neutrality and easy migration. Most of the services are implemented using platform-independent languages (e.g., Java) and are hosted in the platform-independent containers. The main issue then becomes not so much OS support for migration, as for independent evolution of different parts of the systems. One of the serious problems of synchronous (RPC) distributed systems is the requirement for coordinated evolution of clients and servers. In a closed RPC environment such evolution is comparatively easy: a notification that API is going to change is sent and all clients are updated accordingly. It is clear that such strategy will not work in the SOA world, because data model is not shared and not all needs can be communicated directly in advance. Synchronous and named communication is poorly suited to that scenario. Therefore, OS support for independent evolution by enforcing asynchronous, loosely coupled and anonymous process communication is essential. That way, independent evolution on both sides (clients and services) can be performed with minimal shared understanding.

2.4 Possible OS Architectures

Let us examine possible architectures that are available for the construction of dependable service-oriented operating system. OS design has historically developed over monolithic OS, layered OS, virtual machine concept, exokernel and client-server OS. Apart from that, the major distinction is also the resource domain: single processor machine, multiprocessor machine, the network or a distributed system. While one can argue that there is not much difference between single processor OS and network

OS, distributed OS and accompanying middleware have special properties such as communication delays, incomplete and/or outdated information and incorrect data. Service-oriented OS can be designed as both single/multiprocessor OS (running on a single machine) or as a distributed OS. It also may turn out that the best solution is in the middle: some actors of SOC landscape may execute inside distributed OS (e.g., shared business logic or service implementations), while databases may run in their native OS.

Monolithic design is easily mapped into SOC principles, with main kernel procedure calling OS (kernel) services, which are in turn not self-contained, as they themselves call OS utilities. The main problems with this design are dependability and security: everything (including device drivers) is executing inside kernel, and with service-oriented OS other middleware elements will be also executing inside the kernel. This presents a big security challenge. Instead of monolithic design, layered design can be proposed, where process at layer $k+1$ does not have to worry about the issues solved (provided by) previous layers $1..k$. Security problems in this architecture can be solved by introducing levels of priorities (e.g., rings like in MULTICS) that are supported by hardware. This architecture also easily maps to the layers presented in Figure 3: native, composed and managed services. Another aspect of SOC that was mentioned is server consolidation though virtualization. There are several virtualization methods, belonging roughly into either providing exact copy of the same machine (e.g., VMWare or Virtual PC), or the copy of a different machine (e.g., Solaris Zones). To be more precise, virtualization can be performed at the instruction set, hardware abstraction layer, operating system, library or application level. Introducing virtualization in the service-oriented OS concept helps not only server consolidation, but addresses the problems of security (isolation) and kernel debugging and driver development. Further in that direction is also a concept of exokernel, which is a virtual machine with the subset of resources of the original machine. This idea is also in line with the problem of fine grained resource control: process has no illusion that resources are abstracted; quite on the contrary, it is implicitly aware that resources are constrained. Client-server OS design is based on the idea of a microkernel: clients as well as OS services run in user mode, and communicate using IPC through microkernel. Kernel comprises only interrupts, process management, scheduling and IPC, while all other OS services run as servers in user mode (e.g., file server). This architecture is almost inherently service-oriented, and it also offers security advantages since all drivers and potentially damaging code are removed from the kernel. The well-known problem is the performance of such OS. However, according to [17] for some test cases the overhead was under 10%. Finally, introducing contracts for microkernel services may lead to a speculation that design and runtime verification can be potentially performed. Coming back to the issue of single machine OS/distributed OS, in the former case the big challenge is to enable IPC, and in the latter to ensure consistency.

Design of dependable service-oriented OS presents some unique research challenges and requires mastering an entire spectrum of problems. In order to summarize the issues presented, an orthogonal OS design methodology is presented. The dimensions of the design are 1) OS is a set of collaborating kernel services; 2) OS should support services present in the current SOA middleware and 3) OS should support relevant properties (dynamic client-server interaction, dependability, prediction, security, self-*, migration, trust). Aspects of separate problem domains such as task scheduling, stream processing strategies or memory management are found in the intersection of the three dimensions (Figure 5). Performance is orthogonal to all given dimensions.

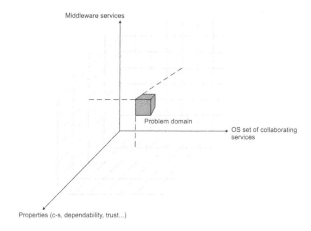

Fig. 5. Orthogonal design

3   Conclusion

We are entering the era of distributed computing where service availability is becoming the dominating requirement, and where multiple services will be contending for the clients at the service marketplace. The ideas, principles and a framework proposed in this paper enable systematic design of a new type of dependable OS which is specifically tailored to enhance availability of modern service-oriented applications. It does so by considering peculiarities of SOA-based systems and providing supporting mechanisms at the OS level which enable not only a robust OS design but also enhance service availability, reliability, integrity and maintainability.

References

[1] S. Burbeck. The Tao of e-business Services, Emerging Technologies, IBM Software Group, ftp://www6.software.ibm.com/software/developer/library/ws-tao.pdf, 2000.
[2] D.A. Chappel. *Enterprise Service Bus*, O'Reilly Media Inc., 2004.
[3] P. W. Chan, M. R. Lyu and M. Malek, *Making Services Fault Tolerant,* Service Availability, D. Penkler, M. Reitenspiess and F. Tam (eds.), Lecture Notes in Computer Science, LNCS 4328, Springer Verlag, 2006.
[4] D. Gelernter, Generative Communication in Linda. *Communications of the ACM*, 7(1), 1985.
[5] G. Hoffmann and M. Malek, *Call Availability Prediction in a Telecommunication System: A Data Driven Empirical Approach,* 25th IEEE Symposium on Reliable Distributed Systems (SRDS 2006), Leeds, UK, October 2006.

[6] G. Hoffmann, K. S. Trivedi and M. Malek, *A Best Practice Guide to Resource Forecast-ing for the Apache Webserver,* 12th IEEE International Symposium Pacific Rim Depend-able Computing (PRDC'06), University of California, Riverside, USA, December 2006.

[7] W3C Working Group. Web Services Architecture. *http://www.w3.org/TR/ws-arch/,* 2004.

[8] D. Krafzig, K. Banke, and D. Slama. *Enterprise SOA: Service-Oriented Architecture Best Practices.* Prentice Hall PTR, 2004.

[9] Doug Lea, Steve Vinoski, and Werner Vogels. Asynchronous Middleware and Services. *IEEE Internet Computing,* 10(1):14–17, 2006.

[10] M.R. Lyu and A. Avizienis. Assuring Design Diversity in N-Version Software: A Design Paradigm for N-Version Programming, in Proceedings 2nd IEEE International Working Conference on Dependable Computing for Critical Applications, Tucson, Arizona, Feb-ruary 18-20 1991, pp. 89-98.

[11] Brian Randell, "System structure for software fault tolerance." *IEEE Transactions on Software Engineering,* Vol. SE-1, No. 2, June 1975, pp. 220-232.

[12] A. S. Tanenbaum, J.N. Herder, and H. Bos. Can We Make Operating Systems Reliable and Secure? *IEEE Computer,* 39(5):44–51, 2006.

[13] A.S. Tanenbaum and A.S.Woodhull. *Operating Systems: Design and Implementation.* Prentice Hall, 2006.

[14] M. Welsh and D. Culler. Virtualization considered harmful: OS design directions for well-conditioned services. In *Proceedings of the 8th Workshop on Hot Topics in Operat-ing Systems,* 2001.

[15] M.Schoebel. Operating System Abstractions for Service-based Systems, *Proceedings of the Fall 2006 Workshop of the HPI Research School on Service-oriented Sys-tems Engineering,* Technical Report 18, HPI, University of Potsdam, 2007.

[16] A. Avizienis, J.-C. Laprie, B. Randell, C. Landwehr. Basic Concepts and Taxonomy of Dependable and Secure Computing, *IEEE Transactions on Dependable and Secure Com-puting,* vol. 01, no. 1, pp. 11-33, Jan-Mar, 2004.

[17] J. N. Herder, H. Bos, B. Gras, P. Homburg and A. S. Tanenbaum, Robustness and Fault Tolerance Design of a Highly Dependable Operating System, *In Proceedings of 6th European Dependable Computing Conference (EDCC-6),* Coimbra, Oct. 2006.

Implementation
of Highly Available Memory Database
as SAF Component

Tadashiro Yoshida, Masaki Hisada, and Seiji Tomita

Nippon Telegraph and Telephone Corporation,
1-1 Hikari-no-oka, Yokosuka, Kanagawa, 239-0847 Japan
{yoshida.tadashiro,hisada.masaki,tomita.seiji}@lab.ntt.co.jp

Abstract. This paper describes the implementation of a highly available memory database with HA (High Availability) middleware based on the SAF (Service Availability™ Forum) specification. The database achieves high availability in conjunction with AMF and MSG in a loosely coupled cluster. We describe its startup and re-synchronization methods; they reduce service interruption and system downtime, and are significant determiners of the availability of the shared-nothing architecture. To further enhance availability, we describe an additional SAF-AIS interface that accepts request from components.

Keywords: memory database, high availability and reliability, loosely coupled architecture, active and hot standby, synchronization.

1 Introduction

SIP-VoIP and Open Source Software technology have considerably influenced the development of telecommunication systems that must offer high availability and reliability. Conventional systems are implemented with specially-designed hardware and software including operating systems and high availability middleware, which counters the trend of continuous cost reduction. The telecommunications industry is energetically tackling the migration to NGN (Next Generation Network) [1],[2],[3] and 3GPP IMS (IP Multimedia Subsystems)[4], both of which are expected to reduce costs and provide new services through FMC (Fixed Mobile Convergence)[5] and ICT (Information and Communication Technology).

The open architecture is a necessity because NGN is tasked with achieving the same service quality (connectivity, voice quality, and reliability) as the conventional network but at much lower cost. It can also provide flexibility since its components can be altered to implement additional services. Therefore, products, such as general-purpose hardware, operating systems, and HA (high availability) middleware, based on ATCA (Advanced Telecom Computing Architecture) [6], CGL (Carrier Grade Linux) [7], and SAF (Service Availability™ Forum) [8], represent one of the most promising solutions.

The memory database is a key component of telecommunication systems [14]. It provides applications with high performance and reliable data access, and enables

M. Malek et al.(Eds.): ISAS 2007, LNCS 4526, pp. 43–51, 2007.
© Springer-Verlag Berlin Heidelberg 2007

rapid and cost-saving application development because application developers do not have to be bothered with complicated operations such as concurrency control, recovery, and so on. In the shared nothing and active/hot standby architecture [9], data synchronization between the databases in each node, to assure availability, is an indispensable and crucial function since it allows a failed database to be rapidly replaced by its standby, as well as recovery of the basic database function within a single environment.

Section 2 describes a system overview of the proposed memory database running as an SAF SA-Aware component. Section 3 explains two functions, re-synchronization of databases and startup for establishing an active database, both which are unique to the shared nothing architecture of the proposed database and contribute to achieving 99.999% availability. Section 4 evaluates one implementation. Finally, Section 5 describes future works and our conclusions.

2 Design Overview

Although modern memory databases offer their own high availability functions, performance can be easily enhanced by using HA middleware based on the SAF-AIS specification to yield the cluster architecture. AMF's prompt error handling functions, moreover, can increase the availability of the entire system.

2.1 Memory Database

The memory database proposed here offers the basic functions of traditional DBMS (Data Management System) [11],[12], such as transaction management, concurrency control, recovery management, and so forth. It also provides a data access method based on SQL-92 and SQL/CLI (Call Level Interface).

Its architecture is specialized to suit telecommunication systems, and achieves real-time response and high availability [14],[15]:

- Disk I/O is prevented as much as possible by storing data in memory; a snapshot of the memory image and transaction logs are written to disk for recovery.
- Data manipulation functions are linked as a library and executed in an application process, which reduces communication cost between application and database components. Note that the database component has other processes for recovery and status control.
- Snapshots are recorded at regular intervals and/or when the transaction log exceeds a threshold, which shortens the restoration time spent patching the transaction logs to the loaded snapshot.

2.2 Cooperation with HA Middleware

Fig. 1 provides a design overview of the highly available memory database as an SA-Aware component. Several modules in the memory database component greatly contribute to increasing availability through their cooperation with SAF AMF (Availability Management Framework) Area Server.

Furthermore, a replication-based redundant database can be easily realized by using the MSG (Message Service) Area Server, which is superior to the shared-disk architecture in terms of availability; the shared-disk architecture needs disk syncing when switching over to ensure data consistency between nodes.

2.2.1 Database Monitor

Database Monitor is the main module; it controls the status of the memory database component. It also performs the role of monitoring modules in the database, reporting failure to AMF, and so forth. Functions related to SAF area servers are as follows:

- Receiving system request to change component's HA state such as "Active/Standby/Quiescing" from AMF, and starting/closing database components as requested.
- Asking AMF for passive process monitoring of the Database Monitor; Other processes in the database component are already monitored by Database Monitor, not AMF.
- Replying to health check requests from AMF. Health checks of sub threads are also executed in each process of the database components independently and asynchronously in response to each health check from AMF.
- Reporting failure to AMF using Component Error Report interface. When a problem occurs in any process and/or thread in the database component, Database Monitor detects it and reports same to AMF.
- Getting address information of nodes in the cluster through CLM to check the status of other databases as described in 3.2.

2.2.2 Transaction Logger and Standby Monitor

Transaction Logger writes updated information into a hard disk in own node at every transaction, which ensures the atomicity and consistency of the database.

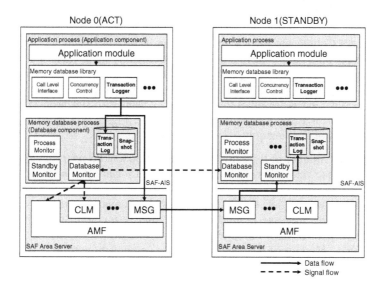

Fig. 1. Design Overview of Highly Available Memory Database

It also sends these logs to other nodes by using MSG functions so that the databases in a cluster can synchronize to each other to achieve quick failover when an active node fails. Although MSG provides three types of sending functions, the newly developed memory database uses the Synchronous Sending method, which can completely prevent data loss between nodes and so maintain the performance of the active database.

Standby Monitor in the standby node extracts transaction logs from the MSG queue after getting notification from MSG, and applies it to the standby database asynchronously, in terms of time.

3 Increasing Availability in Shared-Nothing Architecture

Active and standby database components should be synchronized at all times for quick switchover/failover in the shared-nothing architecture. When starting, the active database component loads data from own disk, while the standby loads data from the active node to realize synchronization. After initial synchronization, the active and standby databases maintain synchronization by passing transaction logs as described in 2.2.2.

3.1 Re-synchronization Between Active and Standby Databases

When the active database component can not send logs for a certain period of time due to a problem with the network between nodes or the standby node, it stops sending them to maintain realtime response to and good concurrency for the active application. This can cause fatal inconsistency between the active and the standby databases, especially if the network problem is intermittent; re-synchronization must be reestablished as soon as possible.

The active database component should inform AMF of this situation at once because AMF controls the active/standby HA state of components. AMF, however, does not have any interface that could accept any request to change HA state of the components except Component Error Report, nor can it restrain switching over the components. Meanwhile, the standby database can not identify the asynchronous situation by itself because it can not distinguish failure from no transaction, when messages are not received.

The proposed database resolves this problem by using "Re-synchronize" messages and the Component Error Report interface of AMF. Fig. 2 and the following text describe the flow of this function:

1. Database Monitor of the active database component keeps trying to send "Re-synchronize" messages once it determines that it can not send transaction logs to the standby.
2. Standby Monitor of the standby database component receives the "Re-synchronize" message from MSG queue after restoration, and notifies receipt of same to its Database Monitor.
3. Database Monitor of the standby database component notifies AMF to restart components by using Component Error Report.
4. AMF in the standby node restarts components.
5. (Regular processes for starting as standby are then performed)

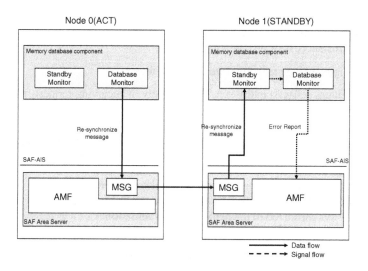

Fig. 2. Architecture for Re-synchronization

This method is useful in two ways. One is that the system can be implemented completely according to the SAF-AIS specification. The other is that the database components can re-synchronize without AMF, although AMF would be used to restart components that abide by the SAF-AIS specification.

3.2 Reduction of Time to Establish Active Node

Establishing any active node as soon as possible, when all nodes are down, is crucial to realize 99.999% availability. Note that 99.999% availability means that downtime is less than approximately 5 minutes a year.

When all nodes start up at almost the same time, AMF decides to assign active state to the node whose components complete instantiation first. The database component, thereafter, begins loading data after receiving a request assigning it to be active from the AMF in the node. The database in the node selected to be standby has to wait until the completion of loading in the active node for replication. This takes quite a long time since it involves disk I/O. If the activating database fails during loading, AMF gives it up and assigns the active state to another node. In this situation, it takes longer, at worst twice the usual time, to establish an active node, and availability is decreased as a result.

One effective solution is for all databases to preload data from own disk in the instantiating phase until one database becomes fully active. The database component checks the status of other databases independently from SAF area servers, and decides which HA state is likely to be given by AMF.

Process flow of Database Monitor upon instantiation is as follows:

1. Checks the status of the other databases.
2. (a) Decides to become active and loads data from own disk, if no active database exists. (called "Temporary Active")

(b) Decides to become standby and loads data from the active, otherwise. (called "Temporary Standby")

3.   Returns success of instantiation to AMF.

(AMF assigns active / standby state to the database)

4.   (a) Enters active/standby state immediately, if receiving request from AMF to become active or standby in "Temporary Active" or "Temporary Standby", respectively.
(b) Pops loaded data and synchronizes to the active database, if receiving request to become standby in "Temporary Active", which means another database in the cluster has become active first.
(c) Turns active, if receiving request to become active in "Temporary Standby". Remember that the database in the Temporary Standby has been already synchronized to the active after instantiation.

It might be useful if AMF had an interface that could return the status of specific components in another node so that the components would omit to implement these communication functions.

4   Implementation and Evaluation

This section describes our evaluation of the functions used to increase availability in the 2N (act/hot standby) loosely coupled architecture [9],[10]. The platform used Intel® Xeon™ 2.80GHz x 2, DIMM Synchronous 400 MHz 4GB memory, 300GB 10KRPM hard disk with writeback mode, enhanced CGL OS [7],[13] based on Redhat® Enterprise Linux4 (kernel 2.6.9-5.EL.smp #1 SMP), HA middleware [8],[13] and the memory database developed in our laboratories. Two nodes were connected by a Gigabit Ether Channel. For simplicity, the database was the only component running on the AMF's SU (Service Unit); a stress tool was run outside of the SU. 1GB of data used in the SIP-VoIP applications was stored in the disk.

4.1   Results: Replication Overhead

We measured the overhead of replication associated with transmitting the transaction log, triggered by insert/update/delete operations, to a standby node as compared to a standalone system. Table 1 shows the average response time of the 1000 tps update transaction using one of the tables and a simple SIP application query, to compare the standalone system and the act/hot standby system.

Table 1. Replication Overhead

	Updating database space (usec)	Operation on transaction log (usec)	Response (usec)
(a)Standalone	45	133	181
(b)Act/hot Standby	49	490	543
Ratio ((b)/ (a))	108.9%	368.4%	300.0%

Replication took approximately 350 usecs, which is about 2.5 times as long as the operation writing transaction logs into the disk within the standalone. As a result, the act/hot standby had three times longer response time than the standalone.

We note that the status of applications and database can become inconsistent if trouble occurs during the commit operation. For instance, if trouble occurs just after writing transaction logs into the disk and before returning success response to the application, the database loads transaction logs when re-starting although the application believes that the former operation failed. A similar problem exists in the act/hot standby architecture, if the trouble occurs between right after transmitting transaction logs but before returning success response to the application. The application (or transaction monitor) should have a current transaction ID, and check it with one in the database right after failover.

4.2 Detecting Inconsistency Between Active and Standby Databases

The standby database is inconsistent against the active after recovery from network trouble until AMF detects the error report as described in 3.1. Fig. 3 plots this period versus transaction load in the active database; a simple single update query is used as a transaction. The diamonds and bars in Fig. 3 represent average values and range, respectively.

It takes 1-2 seconds on average to detect inconsistency, while the range of detection time is increases slightly with transaction load. That the detection time initially remains constant is apparently due to MSG's priority control; the "Re-synchronize" message is executed with top priority. At high loads, extracting the "Re-synchronize" degrades detection performance because it takes longer to patch the large quantity of the extracted transaction logs to the standby database, which triggers disk I/O to store transaction logs in the standby, before extracting the "Re-synchronize" message.

Taking several seconds to detect data inconsistency is fatal for realtime applications because hundreds of update transactions could be executed before detection. Thus, it is strongly recommended that AMF be given an interface that can receive requests from components since this would provide more rapid control of node status.

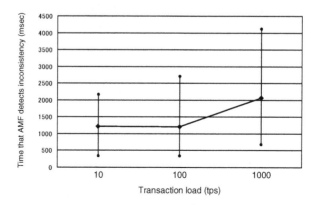

Fig. 3. Detection of Database Inconsistency

4.3 Time to Establish Active Node

Fig. 4 shows the model used in the experiment to assess starting, in which node 1 is instantiated 1 second after node 0; the parameter is the time between instantiation and trouble occurrence in node 0. Fig. 5 depicts the results of the experiment. It shows that the time taken to establish the active node is almost constant, despite the network trouble, due to the function described in 3.2. For reference, the response in the "no trouble" condition is plotted in the rightmost column. Note that total time for activation depends on the data size of the database.

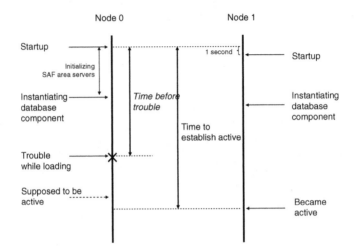

Fig. 4. Model for Startup Check

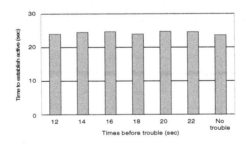

Fig. 5. Time to Establish Active Node

5 Conclusions

We verified through implementation tests that memory databases can have greatly improved availability by being run as an SAF component. The memory database proposed herein can effectively use the process auditing, health checking, and error reporting features provided by AMF for recovery, as well as the messaging function of MSG for replication.

It is crucial to synchronize the active and the standby databases in such a loosely coupled architecture, because they store data independently. This paper also described the features of re-synchronization and shortening the time to establish an active database, which are unique to this architecture. The method described in this paper could be much enhanced by providing AMF with additional interfaces that could receive requests for controlling switchover and determining HA state of components.

Split brain, the situation in which plural active nodes exist in the cluster, is another conceivable problem with this architecture. In most situations, this can be avoided by duplicating the network, i.e. using another reachable communication network such as a service channel [13]. Memory database system, however, should provide tools that arbitrate split brained nodes.

The application of NGN, to realize the information society, has just commenced, and NGN will be enhanced step by step. It is, therefore, important to be able to alter the data scheme of the database as well as the applications without stopping service, while maintaining 99.999 % availability. We believe that most application servers will need to offer even higher availability, as the applications are becoming more important to our lives.

References

1. ITU-T Study Group 13 (Next Generation Networks), http://www.itu.int/ITU-T/studygroups/com13/
2. Promoting NTT Group's Medium-Term Management Strategy, NTT Corporation, 2005,http://www.ntt.co.jp/news/news05e/0511phqg/051109.html
3. 21st century network, BT Group plc, http://www.btplc.com/21cn/
4. 3rd Generation Partnership Project, http://www.3gpp.org/
5. Fixed-Mobile Convergence Alliance, http://www.thefmca.com/
6. Advanced TCA, PCI Industrial Computer Manufacturers Group, http://www.picmg.org/
7. Carrier Grade Linux, OSDL, http://www.osdl.org/lab_activities/carrier_grade_linux/
8. Service Availability Forum, http://www.saforum.org/
9. Sam Drake et al.: Architecture of Highly Available Database, Proc. of International Service Availability Symposium (ISAS 2004). In: Lecture Notes in Computer Science, Vol 3335, pp.1-16, Springer-Verlag (2005)
10. A.Wolski, B.Hofhauser: A Self-Managing High-Availability Database: Industrial Case Study, Proceedings of the 21st International Conference on Data Engineering (ICDE '05)
11. H.G.Molina, H.D.Ullman, J.Widom, Database Systems: The Complete Book, Prentice Hall (2002)
12. R.Ramakrishnan, J.Gehrke: Database Management Systems, McGrawHill (2003)
13. H.Shina, T.Ikebe, M.Kaneko: Carrier-Grade Server Architecture for Next-Generation Network, Proceedings of World Telecommunications Congress 2006, CW1-3 (2006)
14. J. Baulier et al.,: DataBlitz storage manager: main-memory database performance for critical applications, ACM SIGMOD Record, Vol.28, Issue 2, pp.519-520 (1999)
15. CORPORATE TimesTen Team: In-Memory Data Management for Consumer Transactions The TimesTen Approach, Proceedings SIGMOD '99 international conference on Management of data, pp.528-529 (1999)

Fault Tolerant Schemes for Hot-Swappable and Non Hot-Swappable Mezzanine Cards

Mark Lanus

Availability Engineering Department, Motorola Embedded Communications Computing,
2900 S. Diable Way, DW220,
Tempe AZ, USA 85282
mark.lanus@motorola.com

Abstract. First generation, highly-available computer systems deployed a two-level physical hierarchy whereby a shelf was composed of field replaceable units (FRU) and the unit of fault detection, fault isolation, fault containment, fault recovery, fault repair, and sparing was the FRU. In 1995, IEEE introduced the non hot-swappable PCI Mezzanine Card (PMC) draft standard [1] that allows fault detection, isolation, containment, recovery, and sparing to be implemented at the mezzanine card level but requires fault repair to occur at the carrier board level. In 2005 the PCI Industrial Computer Manufacturers Group (PICMG®) introduced the hot swappable Advanced Mezzanine Card (AMC) standard [2] that extends the PMC model to allow all fault management functions, including fault repair, to be implemented at the mezzanine card level. This paper develops fault management strategies and availability models for the monolithic, non hot swap partitioned, and hot swap partitioned hardware architectures.

Keywords: Availability Model, Fault Management Model, Advanced Mezzanine Card, AMC, AMC Carrier, PCI Mezzanine Card, PMC, PMC Carrier.

1 Introduction

The evolution of modular hardware architecture from monolithic boards, to non hot-swappable PMC mezzanine cards [1], to hot-swappable AMC mezzanine cards [2] described in the abstract suggests the following fault management strategies for carrier/mezzanine assemblies.

Monolithic: A carrier or mezzanine failure causes the carrier and all mezzanines to failover to the redundant carrier/mezzanine assembly and the failed assembly is replaced.

Non Hot swap Partitioned: A mezzanine failure causes only that mezzanine to failover to the redundant carrier/mezzanine assembly. When the craft arrives to repair the failed mezzanine, the carrier and all unfailed mezzanines are switched over to the redundant assembly and the failed assembly is replaced. A carrier failure causes the carrier and all mezzanines to failover to the standby assembly and the failed assembly is replaced.

Hot swap Partitioned: A mezzanine failure causes only that mezzanine to failover to the redundant carrier/mezzanine assembly. When the craft arrives to repair the failed

M. Malek et al.(Eds.): ISAS 2007, LNCS 4526, pp. 52–62, 2007.
© Springer-Verlag Berlin Heidelberg 2007

mezzanine, the mezzanine is replaced without impacting the unfailed mezzanines. A carrier failure causes the carrier and all mezzanines to failover to the standby assembly and the failed assembly is replaced.

These fault management strategies are *backward compatible*. A monolithic hardware module can only implement the monolithic strategy, a non hot swap partitioned module can implement either the monolithic or non hot swap partitioned strategy, and a hot swap partitioned module can implement any strategy. Even though the hardware architecture supports a more sophisticated fault management strategy, the system integrator may decide to deploy a simpler strategy due to software complexity, human factors considerations, or sparing policies.

Motivation for performing this work was based on the development of the Motorola AXP-1600 and AXP-1406 AdvancedTCA products. These backplane-based systems consisted of blades for switching, blades for payload processing, and modules for shelf management, system management, clock distribution, fan control, and power entry. One question that arose in the development was, "What is the difference in availability if we move the system management module from a PMC module on the switch blade to an AMC module on the switch blade?" Another question was, "What is the impact on availability if we move from a four processor monolithic payload blade to a payload blade based on an AMC carrier and four AMC processor modules?" This modeling work enabled Motorola to answer these questions and base our decisions on a quantifiable approach.

2 Block Diagram

Figure 1 shows a block diagram for a PMC carrier/mezzanine assembly, showing N mezzanines (Mezz 1..Mezz N), a small amount of logic to support each mezzanine (Sup 1..Sup N), and a large amount of logic to support all mezzanines (Carrier). This diagram models a carrier whose entire purpose is to support the mezzanines and does not model a carrier that provides service independent of the mezzanines. Figure 2 also shows a block diagram for an AMC carrier/mezzanine assembly—the only difference being that the mezzanines are shown external to the carrier as they are independently hot-swappable.

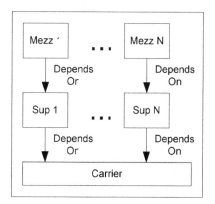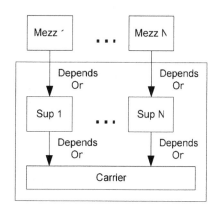

Fig. 1. N-Wide PMC and AMC Carrier Block Diagrams

3 Fault Management Strategies

Tables 1, 2, and 3 show the detailed monolithic, non hot swap partitioned and hot swap partitioned fault management strategies for Mezz, Sup, and Carrier failures on the active and standby assemblies.

Table 1. Failure Analysis—Monolithic Strategy

HA State	Component	Phase	Action
Active	Mezz	Recovery	Failover all active mezzanines
	Sup Carrier	Repair	Hot swap failed carrier/mezzanine assembly
Standby	Mezz	Recovery	Take all standby mezzanines out of service
	Sup Carrier	Repair	Hot swap failed carrier/mezzanine assembly

Table 2. Failure Analysis—Non Hot swap Partitioned Strategy

HA State	Component	Phase	Action
Active	Mezz Sup	Recovery	Failover failed active mezzanine
		Pre-Repair	Switchover N-1 unfailed active mezzanines
		Repair	Hot swap failed carrier/mezzanine assembly
	Carrier	Recovery	Failover all active mezzanines
		Repair	Hot swap failed carrier/mezzanine assembly
Standby	Mezz Sup	Recovery	Take failed standby mezzanine out of service
		Pre-Repair	Take N-1 unfailed standby mezzanines out of service
		Repair	Hot swap failed carrier/mezzanine assembly
	Carrier	Recovery	Take all standby mezzanines out of service
		Repair	Hot swap failed carrier/mezzanine assembly

Table 3. Fault Analysis—Hot swap Partitioned Strategy

HA State	Component	Phase	Action
Active	Mezz	Recovery	Failover failed active mezzanine
		Repair	Hot swap failed mezzanine
	Sup	Recovery	Failover failed active mezzanine
		Pre-Repair	Switchover N-1 unfailed active mezzanines
		Repair	Hot swap failed carrier/mezzanine assembly
	Carrier	Recovery	Failover all active mezzanines
		Repair	Hot swap failed carrier/mezzanine assembly

Table 3. (*Continued*)

Standby	Mezz	Recovery	Take failed standby mezzanine out of service
		Repair	Hot swap failed mezzanine
	Sup	Recovery	Take failed standby mezzanine out of service
		Pre-Repair	Take N-1 unfailed standby mezzanines out of service
		Repair	Hot swap failed carrier/mezzanine assembly
	Carrier	Recovery	Take all standby mezzanines out of service
		Repair	Hot swap failed carrier/mezzanine assembly

4   Markov Reward Models

Tables 4 and 5 describe parameters and state names used in all models.

Table 4. Markov Model Parameters

Parameter	Description
N	Number of mezzanines on carrier
λ_m	Failure rate of Mezz block
λ_s	Failure rate of Sup block
λ_c	Failure rate of Carrier block
D	Probability of successful detection of failure
F	Probability of successful failover
S	Probability of successful switchover
μ_1	Repair rate of first failure
μ_2	Repair rate of second failure due to unsuccessful switchover in pre-repair
T	Period for exercising diagnostics on standby carrier/mezzanine assembly

Table 5. Markov Model State Names

State Name	Description
Normal	No failure
Act Cov Fail	Covered failure on active assembly
Act Uncov Fail	Uncovered failure on active assembly
Act Rep Fail	Unsuccessful switchover on active assembly in pre-repair
Sby Cov Fail	Covered failure on standby assembly
Sby Uncov Fail	Uncovered failure on standby assembly
Double Fault	Double failure

4.1   Monolithic Model

Figure 2 shows the Markov Reward Model (MRM) [4], [5] for the monolithic fault management strategy. This section describes example state transitions.

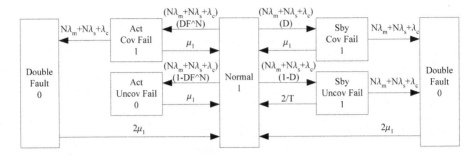

Fig. 2. Monolithic Model

Normal -> Act Cov Fail: Transition from Normal to a covered failure of the active assembly. The failure rate is $N\lambda_m+N\lambda_s+\lambda_c$ as there are N Mezz blocks, N Sup blocks, and one Carrier block to fail. The probability of successful detection is D, the probability of successful failover is F^N (successful failover of N Mezz blocks), so the transition rate is $(N\lambda_m+N\lambda_s+\lambda_c)(DF^N)$. One could argue that, for Mezz or Sup failures, only the failed mezzanine needs to failover, the N-1 unfailed mezzanines can switchover, so the transition rate should be $(N\lambda_m+N\lambda_s)(DFS^{\wedge}(N-1))+\lambda_c DF^N$.

Act Cov Fail -> Double Fault: Transition from Act Cov Fail to the Double Fault state. The failure rate is $N\lambda_m+N\lambda_s+\lambda_c$. (This slightly over-estimates the failure rate for double faults, but allows us to condense three Act Cov Fail states to one.)

Normal -> Sby Cov Fail: Transition from the normal state to a covered failure of the standby unit. The failure rate is $N\lambda_m+N\lambda_s+\lambda_c$ and the probability of successful detection is D. Since this is the standby carrier, failover is not required—only detection.

Sby Uncov Fail -> Normal: Transition from Sby Uncov Fail to Normal. The transition rate is 2/T, where T is the period we run detailed diagnostics to find latent faults on the standby.

Double Fault -> Normal: Transition from Double Fault to Normal. The transition rate is twice the repair rate for first failures. This state is only reached when we are already waiting on a repair action due to a previous failure, the craft is already on the way, and so the repair rate should be faster than the repair rate for first failures.

4.2   Non Hot Swap Partitioned Model

Figure 3 shows the non hot swap partitioned model. The main change from the monolithic model is that the fault management strategy requires different policies for Mezz, Sup, and Carrier failures and so the transition with rate $N\lambda_m+N\lambda_s+\lambda_c$ becomes three transitions with rates $N\lambda_m$, $N\lambda_s$, and λ_c. This section describes a few transitions.

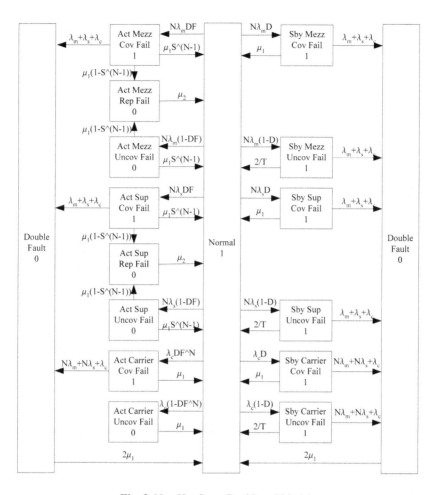

Fig. 3. Non Hot Swap Partitioned Model

Act Mezz Cov Fail -> Normal: The repair rate is μ_1. The pre-repair action is to switchover the N-1 unfailed Mezz blocks and hot swap the carrier/mezzanine assembly. The probability of successful switchover is S^(N-1) so the transition rate is μ_1S^(N-1).

Act Mezz Cov Fail -> Act Mezz Rep Fail: μ_1(1-S^(N-1)) is the product of the repair rate (μ_1) and the probability of a second failure during the pre-repair phase (1-S^(N-1)).

4.3 Hot Swapped Partitioned Model

Figure 4 shows the hot swap partitioned model.

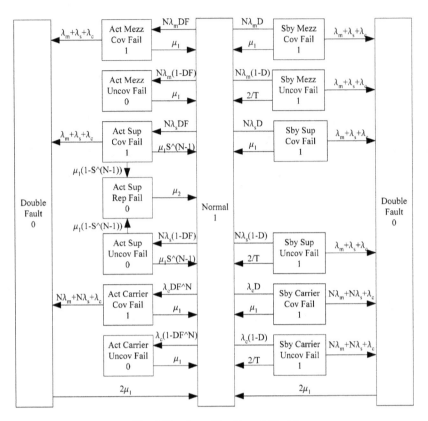

Fig. 4. Hot Swap Partitioned Model

5 Parameters

Table 6 shows the parameter values used in the analysis and rationale for why these numbers were used. The failure rate for AMC modules was originally estimated at 2000 FITs. Recent development indicates that this number should be closer to 700 FITs, but time was not available to update the report with this updated value.

Table 6. Parameter Values

Parameter	Description	Rationale for Parameter Value
N	4	Maximum number of AMCs that fit on ATCA front blade
λ_m	600 FIT	Failure rate estimates of AMC module
λ_s	100 FIT	Failure rate estimates of AMC carrier module
λ_c	1000 FIT	Failure rate estimates of AMC carrier module

Table 6. (*continued*)

D	0.998	Field data analysis of previous systems
F	0.99	Field data analysis of previous systems
S	0.995	Field data analysis of previous systems
μ_1	1/ (4 hour)	Bellcore LSSGR estimate based on field data analysis
μ_2	1 / (1 hour)	Interviews with field engineers on recovery times
T	24 hour	Period at which routine diagnostics are run on real system

6 Results

This section describes modeling results. These results will be verified with field data analysis once the population of fielded systems yields statistically significant data.

Table 7 shows downtime results assuming imperfect detection, failover, and switchover (probability < 1) and perfect detection, failover, and switchover (probability = 1), percent of downtime due to imperfect fault coverage, and the mean time to a failure that causes a system outage. The second row for the monolithic model shows the case where fault recovery consists of one failover for the failed mezzanine and N-1 switchovers for the unfailed mezzanines.

Table 7. Results

Model	Downtime (sec/NE/yr)		Percent Downtime Due to Imperfect Coverage	Mean Time To System Outage (hours)
	Imperfect Coverage	Perfect Coverage		
Monolithic (N failover)	19.8157	0.00728575	99.96%	6,363,580
Monolithic (1 failover, N-1 switchover)	14.6595	0.00728575	99.95%	8,600,720
Non Hot swap Partitioned	10.7661	0.004319	99.96%	8,604,160
Hot swap Partitioned	9.63655	0.004319	99.96%	12,371,200

Table 8 shows the steady-state probability and downtime associated with each state of the monolithic model. Note that only 0.04% of the downtime is due to the *Double Fault* state and 99.96% is due to the *Act Uncov Fail* state.

Table 8. Monolithic Model Results

State	Probability	Downtime (sec/NE/yr)
Normal	9.9997×10^{-1}	0
Double Fault	2.26718×10^{-10}	0.00714979
Act Cov Fail	1.45712×10^{-5}	0
Act Uncov Fail	6.28124×10^{-7}	19.8086
Sby Cov Fail	1.51689×10^{-5}	0
Sby Uncov Fail	9.11931×10^{-8}	0
Total	1.0	19.8157

Tables 9 and 10 show detailed analyses of the non hot swap and hot swap partitioned models. The only difference (1.13 sec/NE/yr) is due to the Act Mezz Rep Fail state of the non hot swap partitioned model, caused by unsuccessful switchover of the N-1 unfailed mezzanines during pre-repair.

Table 9. Non Hot swap Partitioned Model Results

State	Probability	Downtime (sec/NE/yr)
Normal	9.99969 10^-1	0
Double Fault	1.35516 10^-10	0.00427362
Act Mezz Cov Fail	9.48464 10^-6	0
Act Mezz Uncov Fail	1.15004 10^-7	3.62676
Act Sup Cov Fail	1.58077 10^-6	0
Act Sup Uncov Fail	1.91674 10^-8	0.604461
Act Carrier Cov Fail	3.83452 10^-6	0
Act Carrier Uncov Fail	1.65296 10^-7	5.21276
Sby Mezz Cov Fail	9.58044 10^-6	0
Sby Mezz Uncov Fail	5.75971 10^-8	0
Sby Sup Cov Fail	1.59674 10^-6	0
Sby Sup Uncov Fail	9.59951 10^-9	0
Sby Carrier Cov Fail	3.99182 10^-6	0
Sby Carrier Uncov Fail	2.39982 10^-8	0
Act Mezz Rep Fail	3.5819 10^-8	1.12958
Act Sup Rep Fail	5.96983 10^-9	0.188264
Total	1	10.7661

Table 10. Hot swap Partitioned Model Results

State	Probability	Downtime (sec/NE/yr)
Normal	9.9997 10^-1	0
Double Fault	1.35516 10^-10	0.00427364
Act Mezz Cov Fail	9.48464 10^-6	0
Act Mezz Uncov Fail	1.15004 10^-7	3.62677
Act Sup Cov Fail	1.58077 10^-6	0
Act Sup Uncov Fail	1.91674 10^-8	0.604464
Act Carrier Cov Fail	3.83452 10^-6	0
Act Carrier Uncov Fail	1.65296 10^-7	5.21278
Sby Mezz Cov Fail	9.58044 10^-6	0
Sby Mezz Uncov Fail	5.75971 10^-8	0
Sby Sup Cov Fail	1.59674 10^-6	0
Sby Sup Uncov Fail	9.59951 10^-9	0
Sby Carrier Cov Fail	3.99182 10^-6	0
Sby Carrier Uncov Fail	2.39982 10^-8	0
Act Sup Rep Fail	5.96983 10^-9	0.188265
Total	1	9.63655

7 Conclusions

The change from the monolithic to the non hot swap partitioned strategy generates a more significant improvement than the change from the non hot swap to the hot swap partitioned strategy.

The biggest benefit of a partitioned over a monolithic strategy is not the protection against second failures by leaving N-1 mezzanines in redundant mode between fault recovery and repair. The biggest benefit is that the monolithic strategy requires N *immediate failovers* that could cause a *long outage* whereas a partitioned strategy only requires *one immediate failover* that could cause a *long outage* and *0 or N-1 deferred switchovers* that could cause a *much shorter outage*.

The downtime caused by an unsuccessful failover of the N-1 unfailed Mezz/Sup blocks in the monolithic strategy is $N(\lambda_m+\lambda_s)DF(1-F^{\wedge}(N-1))(1/\mu_1)$ which is the time spent in the N-1 Uncov Mezz/Sup Failure state in Figure 5. The interpretation of this equation is that the failure rate of the N Mezz/Sup blocks is $N(\lambda_m+\lambda_s)$ and in order to have unsuccessful failover of the N-1 unfailed Mezz/Sup blocks we first need to detect the failure with probability D and failover the failed Mezz/Sup block with probability F. The probability of unsuccessful failover of the unfailed Mezz/Sup blocks is $1-F^{\wedge}(N-1)$ and the time spent repairing the second failure is $(1/\mu_1)$. The downtime caused by an unsuccessful switchover of the N-1 unfailed Mezz/Sup blocks in the non hot swap partitioned strategy is $N(\lambda_m+\lambda_s)DF(1-S^{\wedge}(N-1))(1/\mu_2)$ so a good approximation of the downtime improvement from the monolithic to the non hot swap partitioned strategy is $N(\lambda_m+\lambda_s)DF[(1-F^{\wedge}(N-1))(1/\mu_1)-(1-S^{\wedge}(N-1))(1/\mu_2)]$.

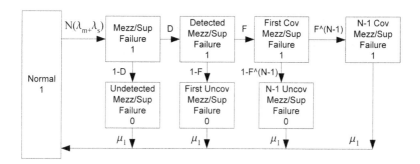

Fig. 5. Downtime due to Unsuccessful Failover of N-1 Unfailed Mezzanines

The biggest improvement from a non hot swap to a hot swap partitioned strategy is that after a mezzanine failure the non hot swap partitioned strategy must eventually switchover the N-1 unfailed mezzanines whereas the hot swap partitioned strategy does not require any switchover. A good approximation of the downtime improvement from the non hot swap to the hot swap partitioned strategy is $N(\lambda_m+\lambda_s)DF(1-S^{\wedge}(N-1))(1/\mu_2)$.

This analysis models quantifiable parameters like failure rate, failover probability, switchover probability, and repair rate. However, there are other issues that should be considered when selecting a fault management strategy for partitioned modules;

Software Simplicity: While the monolithic strategy has the drawback of requiring extraneous failovers, it has the benefit of simplicity of software implementation.

Human Factors/Sparing Strategy: Consider questions such as "If a mezzanine fails, do we ship a mezzanine or a complete carrier/mezzanine assembly?" and "If a carrier fails, do we ship a replacement carrier and require the craft to move unfailed mezzanines from the failed carrier to the replacement, or ship complete a complete carrier/mezzanine assembly?" These impact the type and number of spare parts required, human error downtime due to overly-complex repair procedures, and the No Trouble Found (NTF) rate due to returning a failed assembly containing unfailed subassemblies.

Signaling Complexity: PICMG 3.0 [3] specifies LEDs on carriers to signal the In Service and Fault states of the carrier. PICMG AMC.0 [2] specifies similar LEDs on AMC modules. The more complex partitioned strategies complicate signaling requirements and could increase downtime due to human error caused by overly-complex signaling.

References

1. IEEE, IEEE Std 1386.1-2001, IEEE Standard Physical and Environmental Layers for PCI Mezzanine Cards (PMC), Approved 14 June 2001.
2. PICMG AMC.0 R1.0, Advanced Mezzanine Card Base Specification, January 3, 2005.
3. PICMG R3.0 Revision 2.0, AdvancedTCA Base Specification, March 18, 2005. R. Sahner, K. Trivedi, A. Puliafito, Performance and Reliability Analysis of Computer Systems, An Example-Based Approach Using the SHARPE Software Package, Kluwer Academic Publishers, 1996.
4. G. Bolch, S. Greiner, H. de Merr, K. Trivedi, Queueing Networks and Markov Chains, Modeling and Performance Evaluation with Computer Science Applications, John Wiley and Sons, Inc., 1998.
5. Bellcore, LSSGR: Reliability, Section 12, Generic Requirements GR-512-CORE, Issue 2, January 1998.

Experience in Developing a High Availability and Continuous TCP Using OpenAIS and TCPCP

Ying-Yu Chen[1], Chien Chen[2], and Chia-Yuan Huang[1]

[1] Information & Communications Research Laboratories,
Industrial Technology Research Institute,
195 Chung Hsing Rd., Sec. 4, Chu Tung, Hsinchu 310, Taiwan
{itri404393,ricehuang}@itri.org.tw
[2] Department of Computer Science, National Chiao Tung University,
Hsinchu, Taiwan, R.O.C
cchen@cis.nctu.edu.tw

Abstract. It has become one of the basic requirements for the service providers to deliver highly available services to meet the customers' critical needs. However, a highly available service does not guarantee that the service is delivered continuously from the user's point of view. In this paper, we share the experience of developing high-availability and continuous TCP using open source OpenAIS and TCPCP/TCPCP2. We describe the main system design for building such systems. We specifically discuss two of the problems that need to be overcome under this kind of design model. For each problem and its corresponding resolution, we show a simulation using ns2 simulator, which provides a deeper insight into the problems for further studies. We also develop a simple application which uses OpenAIS and TCPCP2 to achieve its high availability and service continuity. The results indicate that a high availability and service continuity service can be obtained with minor degradation in performance.

Keywords: High availability, service continuity, TCP, OpenAIS, TCPCP (TCP connection passing).

1 Introduction

As technologies advances, users are getting more and more dependent on network services in their daily lives. Therefore, it is very important that the services delivered to the users are highly reliable and meet the customers' expectation. To achieve high availability, a system usually contains redundant components so that when the main server fails, it can be replaced immediately by another. However, a service with high-availability, e.g., 99.999% uptime, does not guarantee that the service is delivered continuously from the users' point of view. In case where the service has to be transferred from one host to another, e.g. failover and switchover, maintaining service continuity means that the service is transferred with minimal degradation in performance, and without users being aware of it. The properties of possessing high availability and service continuity are referred to as service availability [1].

M. Malek et al.(Eds.): ISAS 2007, LNCS 4526, pp. 63–73, 2007.
© Springer-Verlag Berlin Heidelberg 2007

In this paper, we focus on the failover of TCP connections from one host to another since lots of important network applications are built on top of TCP such as HTTP, FTP, SMTP, SSH, etc. It is hard to make these applications continuous unless the underlying TCP can be made continuous in case of failover. The major challenge is that TCP is a connection-oriented protocol and many of the connection parameters such as sequence number, TCP flags, send/receive buffers, etc., which are kept in the kernel of the active node, have to be synchronized with other standby nodes.

In this paper, we share the experience of developing high availability and continuous TCP using the open source OpenAIS [2] and TCPCP/TCPCP2 [3][4]. We describe how OpenAIS and TCPCP/TCPCP2 can be used to develop services with improved service availability. Then, we elaborate on two problems that occur under this design model. In the case where TCP data flows from the client to the server and a failure occurs within the interval between two checkpoints, one problem arises when the standby server tries to resume the service using the last checkpoint information. Since data that have already been acknowledged have been deleted from the client's TCP send buffer, it is not possible for the client to retransmit those data to the server. One solution is to synchronize TCP acknowledges from servers with checkpoint interval. That is, the acks will only be sent from server every checkpoint interval. However, delaying sending acks from server side would have impact on the TCP throughput. In this paper, the numerical results demonstrate that acks should not be delayed more than 10~40ms depending on the link rates.

The other is about what TCP congestion control status should be set to the standby server when the active server fails, since after all it is the *last* checkpoint information that we use to resume the TCP connections. However, the congestion window size recorded in the last checkpoint may no longer reflect the current network condition. Therefore, we develop a window size prediction method to observe how the performance is affected when a simple mechanism is added to support service availability. The simulation results are shown using ns2 [5] simulator. We also reports the results of a simple application that we developed to observe how the performance is affected when extra overhead is added to support service availability.

The rest of the paper is organized as follows. Section 2 describes how TCP connection passing tools TCPCP/TCPCP2 can be used with OpenAIS to develop service availability services. In Section 3, we describe the problems mentioned above in detail and the respective solutions. The simulation results are shown using ns2 simulator. In Section 4, we show the performance of our simple service availability application. The paper concludes in Section 5.

2 Background and Design Model

2.1 OpenAIS and TCPCP/TCPCP2

OpenAIS is the Linux middleware implementation of the SA Forum's Application Interface Specification (AIS) [6]. SA Forum AIS standardizes the interfaces between SA Forum compliant high availability middleware and service applications so that service availability application software can be developed independent of the underlying platform. Authors in [7] describe the use of Application Management Framework

(AMF) and Checkpoint Service in SA Forum AIS to implement high availability services, where AMF [8] supervises redundant resources within the server cluster to deliver the service with no single point of failure and Checkpoint Service [9] is used to record checkpoint data, which can be retrieved to resume the service after the failure.

TCPCP is the implementation of the mechanism that provides APIs for applications to pass the ownership of TCP connection endpoints from one host to another. TCPCP2 is another form of TCPCP, and is created based on TCPCP. The two are similar in principle and both require the kernel modification in the servers. However, the major advantage over other TCP connection passing methods such as MIGSOCK [10] is that the client side does not have to be modified. Since TCPCP and TCPCP2 are quite similar in nature, for the rest of the paper, the description is based on TCPCP2.

TCPCP2 provides a set of APIs to be used by the application to allow the TCP socket information (SI) (including source/destination IPs and ports, TCP flags, sequence number, send/receive buffer, etc.) to be retrieved/set back from/to the kernel. Therefore, the service process on host A can use TCPCP2 to retrieve SI, and by any means, which is mentioned in Section 2.2, send the retrieved SI to host B. Host B can then set the received SI back to its kernel. Sample procedures to take over the TCP connections can be found in [11]. The APIs provided by TCPCP2 includes:

- **tcpcp_stop( )**. Stop the connected TCP socket form sending and receiving packets.
- **tcpcp_get( )**. Retrieve the TCP socket information.
- **tcpcp_set_si( )**. Set the SI into TCP socket.
- **tcpcp_start( )**. Allow the TCP socket to resume sending and receiving packets.

SA Forum AIS and TCP session takeover are currently included in the OSDL Carrier Grade Linux Requirements and Roadmap [12], respectively.

2.2 Achieving Service Availability

Neither TCPCP nor TCPCP2 describe when to pass the TCP connections or how to transfer the retrieved SI to other hosts. Our approach is to combine the ability of TCPCP2, and the AMF and Checkpoint Service in OpenAIS to achieve our goal. An overview of the design model is shown in Fig. 1.

During normal operation, the application status and TCP SI (retrieved by tcpcp_get( )) of the active server are periodically transferred to the standby nodes in the cluster using the Checkpoint service. When the active fails, the error is detected by the AMF, which then dictate one of the standby nodes to become active. The newly active node can now use the last checkpoint data received from the failed active node to restore the application and TCP status so that it can continue to serve its connected clients. Notice that the ways of redirecting the IP packets which were originally intended for the failed node to the standby node are beyond the scope of this paper. Some references can be found in [13] and [14].

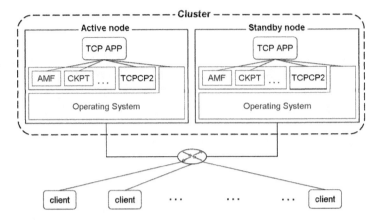

Fig. 1. Design model of a service availability application

3 Problems to Overcome

Despite the simple system design described above, TCP itself is a complicated proto-col and was originally not designed for such usage. Projects of TCPCP and TCPCP2 are still advancing and some problems still leave to be solved [13][15]. In this section, we describe two of them and their corresponding solution, and show the simulation results using ns2 simulator.

3.1 Delaying Acks on Server Side

Consider the situation that the data only flows from the client to the server. Assume that the fail occurs between the last checkpoint and the next checkpoint, as shown in Fig. 2. During the last checkpoint and the fail, the client's TCP may have sent some data with sequence number 4, 5 and 6 out of its send buffer to the server, and the server's TCP may have acknowledged the data in its receive buffer. Therefore, the client will clean the data with sequence number 4, 5 and 6 in its send buffer. The problem arises when the standby server tries to resume the service using the last checkpoint data with sequence number 1, 2 and 3 during a failure, since the client's TCP send buffer contains no data with sequence number 4, 5 and 6. The client is unable to retransmit the data with sequence number 4, 5 and 6 to the server.

A possible solution is to delay the server from sending acks to the client until the server application has retrieved the received data and reached the next checkpoint. That is, the acks will only be sent from server every checkpoint interval. By this it is ensured that even the server fails between checkpoints and the standby server is resumed to the last status, the client's TCP send buffer still contains the data that need to be retrans-mitted. The drawback of such solution is that the estimation of round trip time (RTT) at the client would be affected, which may lead to a TCP throughput degradation.

We simulate the delay acks by modifying ns2 simulator to support this mechanism. A client node and a server node are setup, and between them is a router that forwards the packets from the client to the server. The client keeps sending ftp data to the server.

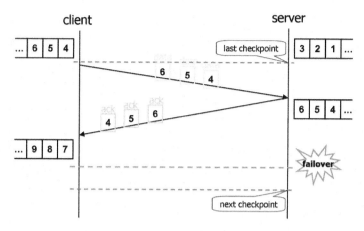

Fig. 2. Illustration for the checkpoint problem when server fails between checkpoints

The throughput is measured under different delay intervals. The results are shown in Fig. 3(a)~3(c), where the link rates are set to 0.5, 1 and 2Mbs, respectively, and the legend on the upper-right corner in each figure is sorted in the sequence of the curves from top to bottom. It is interesting to observe that the throughput does not decrease sharply unless the delay interval is increased to a certain value, and such intense decrease is at least half the throughput of the best curve (i.e., no checkpoint). The results show that the delay acks mechanism degrades the TCP performance significantly

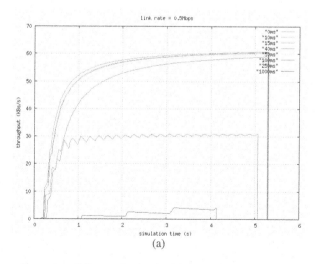

Fig. 3. The throughput when different checkpoint intervals are used. The network link rates are set to 0.5, 1 and 2 Mbps. (a) Link rate = 0.5 Mbps. (b) Link rate = 1 Mbps. (c) Link rate = 2 Mbps.

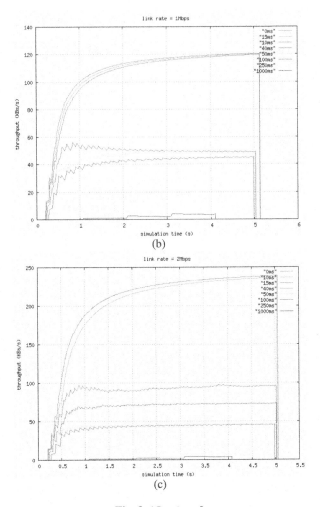

Fig. 3. (*Continued*)

when the acks are postponed more than 40ms, 15ms and 10ms for the link rates 0.5, 1 and 2Mbps respectively. Therefore, the checkpoint interval would have to be bounded within a very small range if delay acks solution is to be applied.

3.2 Congestion Window Prediction

If the failover should happen, the checkpoint data used to resume the service is, after all, not so *fresh*. More specifically, the congestion control data recorded in the SI may no longer reflect the current network condition. Consequently, an improvement may be considered by allowing different strategies to be applied to the congestion control status of the resumed TCP connections.

We conduct the simulation using ns2 and compare the performance when the following strategies are used to set the congestion window size of the resumed TCP connection.

- **slow-start.** Set the congestion window to one.
- **reuse.** Use the congestion window size recorded in the last checkpoint.
- **predict.** Set the congestion window to the well-predicted size.

In this paper, we propose to use the predicted congestion window size by

$$\text{Congestion Window Size}_{predicted} = 1.22/(\text{RTT}*\text{sqrt}(\text{Loss})), \tag{1}$$

which can be simply derived from [16].

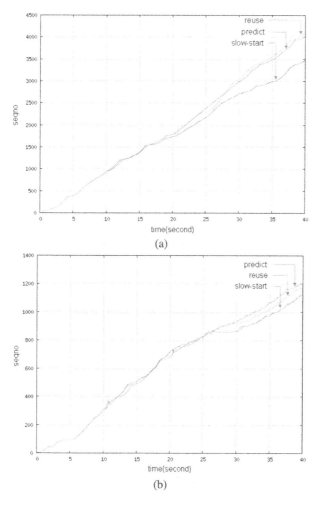

Fig. 4. The growth of sequence vs. time when different congestion window is set to the resumed TCP connection. (a) Delay box loss rate = 0~0.01. (b) Delay box loss rate = 0~0.09.

To simulate the network condition, we put a delay box between the server and the client. The link bandwidth is 2Mbps. The server sends ftp traffic to the client for 40 seconds. At the time 10, 20 and 30 secs, the traffic is interrupted and resumed again. The reuse strategy described above uses the congestion window size retrieved 0.5 sec before the interruption to resume the connection. Figure 4(a) and 4(b) show the comparison results when the loss rate of the delay box is set to 0 ~ 0.01 and 0 ~ 0.09, respectively (in the simulation, a sequence number represents a sent packet). It can be observed that when the loss rate is low (Fig. 4(a)), the slow-start strategy obviously has the slowest growth of sequence number. On the contrary, when the loss rate is high (Fig. 4(b)), the gap between slow-start and the other two is reduced. It can also be observed, although not obvious, that the predict strategy seems to outperform the reuse strategy when the loss rate is high. This is because the higher loss rate also means that the network condition is more unstable. Therefore, a well-predicted congestion window may lead to better performance than reusing the old one.

4   A Simple Service Availability Application

It can be anticipated that tradeoff exits between the degree of service availability and the service performance. The more frequent checkpoint synchronization between active and standby nodes, the less processor time is spent on the original service.

We develop two versions of a simple file transfer program in order to observe the difference in performance, one with the service availability using OpenAIS and TCPCP2, and the other without. The program starts to send a file to the client once the connection is established, and terminates after the completion of the transfer.

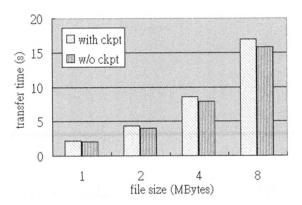

Fig. 5. Comparison of transfer time needed for different file sizes when the program is with and without service availability. The checkpoint interval is set to 0.5 sec.

Figure 5 compares the time needed to transfer files of different sizes to the client, with the checkpoint interval of the service availability version set to 0.5 sec. The result shows that on average, the service availability version takes 6.3% more time than the ordinary version to transfer a file. Figure 6 shows the time needed to transfer an 8Mbytes file to the client, with different checkpoint interval settings. It can be observed that the major decrease in transfer time is when the checkpoint interval is set from 0.1 to 0.2 sec, and the decrease attenuates as the checkpoint interval increases. Figure 7 depicts the growth of sequence number when there are no checkpointing, checkpoint interval = 0.5 sec and checkpoint interval = 0.3 sec, respectively. For the case with checkpoint interval = 0.5 sec (red cross curve), the growth of sequence number is suspended for a tiny moment at 0.5+ sec because the program is retrieving and setting TCP SI. This can also be observed for the case with checkpoint interval = 0.3 sec at 0.6+ sec (green dot curve).

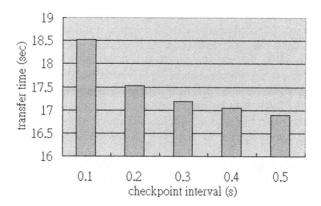

Fig. 6. The time needed to transfer an 8 MBytes file when checkpoint interval is 0.1 ~ 0.5 sec

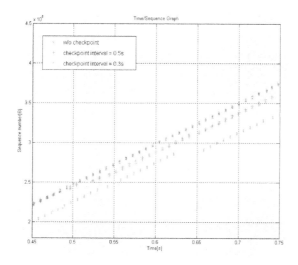

Fig. 7. The growth of sequence number during 0.45 ~ 0.75 sec

5 Conclusion and Future Works

In this paper, we share our experience in developing high availability and continuous TCP using open source OpenAIS and TCPCP/TCPCP2. We show that by delaying sending acks from the server to the client until after the server application has retrieved the received data and finished checkpointing, the data in the client's send buffer can be prevented from being cleared, and thus making TCP recoverable using the last checkpoint. However, the delay can not be too long otherwise the throughput would be severely impaired. We also show that when TCP connections are resumed from the checkpoint data, the congestion window could be well-predicted and set, to improve or preserve the original performance. Even though our simple congestion window prediction function shows minor performance improvement, a more complicated predication function will be invested in the future for further performance improvement. Finally, we display the performance result of a simple file transfer application that uses OpenAIS and TCPCP2 to achieve its service availability. The numerical results show that on average it uses 6.3% more times than the ordinary version to transfer a file when checkpoint is performed every 0.5 second.

The numerical results and the practical implementation presented in this paper provide only a partial inspection on the practicability of service availability TCP-based services. We will further our research on how to strengthen the weaknesses mentioned in [13] and [15], to facilitate the development of robust service availability TCP-based services.

Acknowledgments. We would like to thank Chih-Chiang Yang, Hsin-Fan Chen, Ching-Chun Kao and Lo-Chuan Hu for their support on information about ns2 and programming skills.

References

1. Service Availability Forum. Standards for a Service Availability Solution. http://www.saforum.org/about/solution_backgrounder.pdf
2. http://developer.osdl.org/dev/openais/
3. http://tcpcp.sourceforge.net/
4. http://tcpcp2.sourceforge.net/
5. http://www.isi.edu/nsnam/ns/
6. SA Forum Application Interface Specification AIS B.01.01
7. S. Brossier, F. Herrmann, and E. Shokri. On the Use of the SA Forum Checkpoint and AMF Services. In Proceedings of International Service Availability Symposium 2004 (ISAS 2004), May 2004.
8. SA Forum Application Interface Specification: Availability Management Framework SAI-AIS-AMF-B.01.01
9. SA Forum Application Interface Specification: Checkpoint Service SAI-AIS-CKPT-B.01.01
10. B. Kuntz and K. Rajan. MIGSOCK: Migratable TCP Socket in Linux. Technical Report TR-2001-4, Carnegie Mellon University, Feb. 2002.
11. How to Use TCPCP2.http://prdownloads.sourceforge.net/tcpcp2/how_to_use.pdf?download
12. Open Source Development Labs, Carrier Grade Linux Requirements Definition Documents V3.2. Feb. 2006.
13. W. Almesberger. TCP Connection Passing. In Proceedings of Ottawa Linux Symposium 2004, vol. 1, pp. 9–21, July 2004.

14. F. Leite. Load-Balancing HA clusters with No Single Point of Failure. In Proceedings of the 9th International Linux System Technology Conference (Linux-Congress 2002), pp. 122–131, Sep. 2002.http://www.linux-kongress.org/2002/papers/lk2002-leite.html
15. T. Ikebe, Y. Kawarakaki, and J. Yamanaka. Practical TCP Session Take-over Method for High-availability Network Service. In Proceedings of 6th Asia-Pacific Symposium on Information and Telecommunication Technologies, 2005 (APSITT 2005), pp. 1–6, Nov. 2005.
16. J. Mahdavi and S. Floyd. TCP-Friendly Unicast Rate-Based Flow Control. Technical note sent to the end2end-interest mailing list, January 1997.

Client-Centric Performance Analysis of a High-Availability Cluster

Jesper Grønbæk[1], Hans-Peter Frejek[2], Thibault Renier[1], and Hans-Peter Schwefel[1]

[1] Networking and Security, Department of Electronic Systems
Aalborg University, Fredrik Bajers Vej 7, DK-9220, Aalborg
{ljgr03,tr,hps}@kom.aau.dk
[2] Fujitsu Siemens Computers GmbH
Otto-Hahn-Ring 6, D-81739 München
peter.frejek@fujitsu-siemens.com

Abstract. High-Availability as provided by fault-tolerance mechanisms comes at the price of increased overhead due to additional processing and communication, which may be a limiting factor to service performance as perceived by the clients. In order to quantify this impact and to understand the underlying mechanisms for performance degradation, this paper presents an approach for the analysis of client-centric performance metrics in cluster-based service deployment scenarios using High-Availability Middleware. The approach is based on a combination of measurement based empiric analysis under synthetically generated load patterns and simple queueing models, that allow for the extrapolation of empiric results and are used to gain insights into the underlying causes of the empiric performance behavior. The empiric and numerical results in the paper are based on an abstracted SIP-like call control service as deployed in future version of IP-based cellular networks, running on a two-node cluster system.

1 Introduction

A large part of electronic *end-user services* today rely on being highly available and reliable. Services that cannot meet these high dependability requirements can have a negative impact on user experiences, leading to unnecessary expenses, or in worst case even to critical accidents. To ease the task of developing and deploying services in a highly dependable manner, High-Availability (HA) middleware layer solutions have been emerging on the market to offer generic and standardised interfaces to the *HA services* in the platform [1]. Using these interfaces, an end-user service can be executed in a fault-tolerant manner on top of a cluster architecture, which allows to utilize redundancy while the details are hidden to the end-user service itself. Figure 1 illustrates such an architecture for an end-user service which is accessed by remote clients. In this HA cluster approach, the end-user clients are not aware of the presence or the specific type of utilized fault-tolerance mechanisms, but they can only judge the service quality

M. Malek et al.(Eds.): ISAS 2007, LNCS 4526, pp. 74–93, 2007.
© Springer-Verlag Berlin Heidelberg 2007

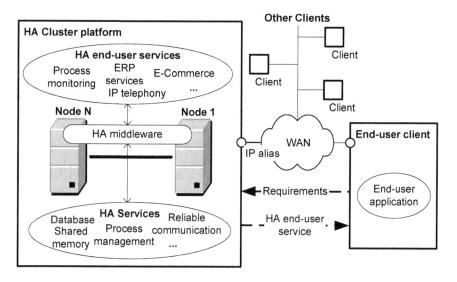

Fig. 1. A HA cluster paradigm supporting a broad range of end user services with requirements for high dependability

by their local perception of the end-user service, typically measured by response times, fraction of successful transactions, or similar metrics.

Providing High-Availability requires additional Hardware and Software, while the latter can reduce or bound achievable performance as perceived by the end-user clients. The performance impact thereby strongly depends on end-user service design choices as well as configuration options of the HA cluster: e.g., which information is stored redundantly in order to be present despite node failures (design decision of end-user service) and how is the redundantly stored information accessed (typical configuration option of the HA middleware, e.g. asynchronously or synchronously).

Consequently, adequate approaches to analyze this performance impact are required to make quantitatively substantiated design decisions during the development of the end-user service as well as during its deployment. Such analysis must consider the end-user service properties, the middleware configuration options and the networking scenario. This paper introduces a methodology for client-centric performance analysis of a cluster-based end-user service and provides performance results for the example of a SIP-type call control end-user service. This service has been chosen due to the relevance of HA Requirements to commercial telco operators, now increasingly moving to IP-based solutions, as emphasized through the ongoing market introduction of the IP-based Multimedia Subsystem (IMS) [2]. Furthermore, such a call control service utilizes certain interesting Middleware functionalities, including replicated data storage, interprocess communication, and communication to end-user clients via dispatchers.

The approach in this paper is based on experimental measurements complemented by analytic models: the experimental measurements are obtained from syntheticly generated load (incoming requests) created in order to mimic large client populations as typical in telco networks. An abstracted version of the call-control end-user service is implemented on top of the HA cluster platform and middleware. The analytic models are based on simple $M/M/1/K$-type queueing models in series with a constant delay stage, which turn out to rather well approximate the experimental system response times. Purpose of the analytic models is to: (1) interpolate and extrapolate performance metrics beyond the measured points of the parameter space (which also includes configuration options), and (2) to obtain insight into the performance relevant mechanisms within the cluster system. Regarding the latter, a detailed inspection of the model properties and the deviations of the predicted performance behaviour leads in the considered example to the adoption of load-dependence service times in the queueing model. Further enhancements can be expected from non-exponential service time distributions. Via the use of Phase-type or Matrix-exponential distributions [3,4], the queueing models thereby stay tractable at low computational complexity. Finally, an outlook on a more complex tandem queueing model, that allows to capture the impact of the specifics of the different individual middleware functionalities is described.

In summary, the main contributions of this paper are: (1) the definition of the overall performance analysis methodology and the identification of a relevant end-user service example. (2) The description of the measurement approach, in particular focusing on load generator and monitoring agents, see Sect. 3. (3) The development of analytic models including the insights obtained from the additional model accuracy at the price of increased complexity, see Sect. 4. (4) The empirical measurement results, which serve for illustration in this paper, but do provide some practical experience to the community nevertheless, see Sect. 5.

2 Performance Analysis Methodology

The methodology developed and applied in this paper uses a combination of experimental measurements and analytic (stochastic) models. The overall approach is outlined in Fig. 2. The performance analysis takes its starting point in a test-scenario. A test-scenario defines performance metrics to evaluate in relation to one or more specific configuration options. Each studied configuration defines a test-case. Considering individual test-scenarios and varying load conditions of the platform, test-cases can be executed while measurements are collected for subsequent off-line analysis. To extrapolate the analysis results and keep the required number of experimental measurement runs low, analytic models are used during the off-line analysis stage.

2.1 Stages in Performance Analysis Methodology

The performance analysis methodology can be described from three main stages:

I - HA end-user service model: The end-user service model is a prerequisite for this performance analysis. It defines which HA services are used in the cluster

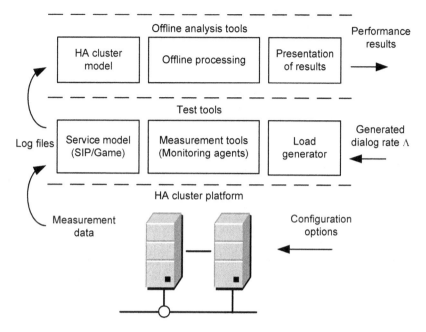

Fig. 2. Overview of the tools constituting the platform for performance analysis

platform and how they are invoked. In addition the model defines service end-user metrics and associated requirements for performance and dependability. This allows system integrators to evaluate how end-user clients are affected given varying configuration options.

In practice the model is used to configure/develop an end-user service implementation used in a measurement platform. Further the model assumptions form the basis for the traffic models in the analytical approach.

II - Performance measurements: Measurement based analysis plays a very important role in the analysis approach. Besides evaluation of performance, the measurements provide a basis to study the behaviour of the platform and the end-user service in operation. This provides useful information to construct and verify models for the analytic approach. In addition basic measurements are needed to parametrize models. As a result this performance analysis method is dependent on a good measurement platform to deliver the desired measurements.

III - Extrapolation analysis: An analytic system model provide means to extrapolate basic measurements to extended analysis cases. Such models encompass the HA cluster system and the HA end-user service. The model abstraction level and type may depend on the performance metrics and HA cluster configurations being studied. The approach in this work is solely based on queueing network models where basic measurements are extrapolated to give HA platform performance metrics under varying load conditions.

2.2   Generic View on Middleware Functionality

The actual experimental analysis, conducted in this work, is executed on a specific HA cluster and middleware platform. However, in order to allow for a generic categorization of end-user services and in order to identify analytic modeling sub-blocks which can be applied generically, a set of basic HA services is identified in this subsection. These HA services are primarily derived from the SAF specifications [1] and the comprehensive HA cluster based platform RTP4CS [5]. In addition other popular HA cluster solutions have been reviewed [6,7,8] for their similarities and differences in terms of offered HA services. While the solutions differ in the amount of functionalities and the methods used to enable them, there are great similarities in the types of services offered to manage the cluster and bring HA to the end-user service. A set of key HA services identified are:

Process Management (PM): Responsible for fault tolerance of service processes running in the cluster.

Process Communication (PC): Enables highly dependable Inter Process Communication (IPC) between processes in the cluster including both node local processes and processes situated in other nodes. Could typically be message based communication.

Context Management (CM): A highly dependable shared memory entity that decouples end-user service data from the end-user services. Enables data to survive a breakdown of the end-user service itself.

Cluster Base (CB): This HA service is responsible for maintaining membership of nodes in the cluster. Further it ensures fault tolerance by monitoring availability of nodes and cluster interconnects to enable recovery operations.

In addition the following service has been considered in relation to RTP.

Dispatchers: Dispatchers are processes used to handle cluster external communication from clients. They are responsible for distributing incoming messages from clients to the processes in the cluster. This functionality may be useful for load balancing and to add support for different high layer protocols.

2.3   HA End-User Service Model Specification

Typical candidate services for High-Availability implementations include transaction-based ticket booking systems, revenue creating entertainment applications like server-based multi-player online games, and telecommunications services. The latter includes SW-based switching and call control implementations. Most of them however operate in a client-server like fashion, in which the requests of the clients trigger some processing and lead to some type of session state which needs to be maintained in a fault-tolerant manner. Hence, all of these application types use similar sets of HA middleware functionality. However, the actual details on e.g. message sizes, communication volumes, and frequency of access to HA middleware interfaces will obviously vary.

Due to their historical relevance for the development of HA middleware, we use a *call control server* as the service example in this paper. As call control in IP-based environments is gaining increasing attention, we use abstracted message flows inspired by the Session Initiation Protocol (SIP) [9] as e.g. used with some variations in IMS [2]. From SIP, a *transaction* can be defined as one request and one or more responses. Additionally, in SIP a *dialog* is defined to describe a sequence of transactions each belonging to the same notion of a session.

To simplify complexity for the preliminary implementation and analysis of the service, in this work a simplified SIP dialog model has been created. Consequently it is referred to as a *SIP-like* end-user service. The server-part of this SIP-like service consists of two processes: A proxy process to handle all dialogs and a location server process providing location information of the clients, here also called User Agents (UA) (See Fig. 8).

The service model is described considering a rough simplification of a call-setup and release dialog including two instant messages being sent. The dialog is depicted in Fig. 3. In case of the INVITE transaction intermediate responses (Trying and Ringing) are not considered. Also in this simplification only two parties are involved in mimicking a caller UA, the HA cluster and the called UA. The four transactions lead to three different job classes in the HA cluster. A *job class* refers to one or more transactions where the same actions are being executed in the HA cluster. In this simple sequence of transactions, actions refer to interprocess communication with a location server process and usage of context management to store dialog states. Clearly, a real deployment of a *call control server* would handle multiple kinds of dialogs with varying requirements for resource and context usage. This should be considered in future work.

As we assume here that the four transactions within a dialog are created in sequence with no intermediate delay on the user-side, only one parameter is required for the traffic model, namely the generated Dialog Rate (DR) 'Λ'.

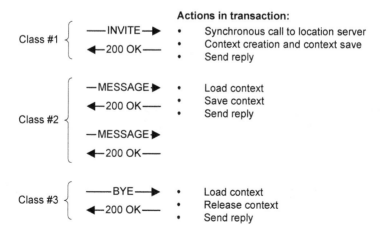

Fig. 3. SIP-like dialog and corresponding HA service actions

It defines the rate at which new dialogs are initiated. Assuming large user populations which independently of each other initiate dialogs, the stochastic process of the dialog initiation instances can be approximated by a Poisson process, which is fully characterized by the single rate parameter.

3   Measurement Platform

To realise performance measurement results from specific performance test-scenarios, means must be established to conduct performance tests. This challenge consists of creating an environment where the HA cluster in a tested configuration can be loaded realistically. Further, measurements must be collected with *low overhead* to minimize the impact on the performance results.

In this work measurements have been considered from an off-line analysis approach. I.e. measurement samples are made during a test period whereafter they are collected centrally for subsequent analysis. In the present case the approach is to define a given configuration, generate measurement data with test tools and process the results subsequently (see Fig. 2). An advantage of the off-line approach is that no CPU resources are required to parse, process and transfer measurements. The cost is typically the amount of memory required to store raw measurements. However memory is considered a cheap resource. Therefore off-line analysis potentially reduces overhead significantly [10].

Measurements are collected by dedicated applications developed in this work called monitoring agents. Agents in each node sample performance variables and store them locally. To ensure that measurements from all nodes are comparable in time all nodes are located in the same NTP synchronized domain. As the measurement platform operates in the same LAN as the used NTP time server a precision in the synchronization of 0.5 ms to 2 ms can be expected for each node [11].

A measurement platform consists of a HA cluster test-bench and a client node. The client node is responsible for mimicking the load from thousands of clients making use of the end-user services in the cluster. Hence it is defined as a *load generator*. These two entities are depicted in Fig. 4.

In this work the SIP-like end-user service is used to define the capabilities of the load generator and also the initial configuration of the HA cluster. The SIP-like end-user services and the SIP-like clients are emulated in the load generator and the cluster by simplified implementations that make use of the HA middleware services and conduct the communication and platform operations in a call setup and release dialog. The SIP-like stub implementations can then be configured to support the test-scenarios to be conducted.

In the execution of a test-scenario the load generator has the role of controlling the measurements in the distributed system. It uses a control channel to send commands to nodes i.e. when to start sampling. The control channel uses the public network but is not active during performance tests. Input to the load generator is the dialog rate 'Λ'. The load generator can then start a test-case

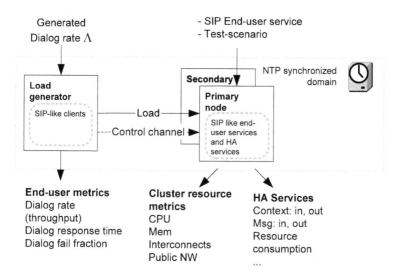

Fig. 4. Measurement platform with NTP synchronized nodes

execution by sending a notification to the cluster nodes to start measurements where after it generates the desired load.

These principles for the measurement platform are general. However, its implementation is specific to the HA cluster being studied. In this work the Fujitsu Siemens Computers (FSC) Reliable Telco Platform (RTP) for Linux has been analysed.

3.1 Generating Load

Load generators need to be able to generate the desired timing behavior (in our case a Poisson process for dialog starts) for the traffic patterns as created by potentially thousands of clients. The emulated clients will be competing for the same resources in the load generator which may impact the resulting traffic patterns. Under these conditions two aims are relevant: *accuracy* and *efficiency*. Accuracy of the load generator is important to avoid measurements being affected by the load generator itself. Requests should be transmitted as close to their scheduled time as possible to avoid load generator delays adding noise to measurements. Efficiency must ensure that many transactions can be executed concurrently to deliver the required load towards the cluster and avoid the load generator being the bottleneck.

In this work a load generator has been constructed considering these aspects. Resulting design choices have been to (1) avoid high level programming languages where e.g. garbage collectors could affect execution, (2) avoid a threading based design where overhead is introduced for CPU context switching. In addition, inappropriate scheduling and management of concurrent resources may degrade efficiency[12]. Instead an event-driven design has been introduced where a single threaded processing loop handles dialog generation, send, receive, update and time-out events. The challenge is here to schedule the processing of events to avoid delays. In this work an empirical solution has been used to determine a scheduling policy.

In all conducted test-scenarios the load generator has been capable of loading the cluster to its limits. However, the load generator does impose a measurable impact on the dialog response time (DRT). For instance at a rate of 1666 $dialogs/s$ the cluster is averagely loaded to a mean CPU consumption of 55% and average dialog response times are 2165 μs. In this case the delay in the load generator is measured to approximately 160 μs. To compensate for this delay it is subtracted from the measured client-based response times. More on the specific implementation can be found in [13] and some of these principles on load generation are generally discussed in [14].

3.2 Monitoring Agents

As mentioned before performance measurements are gathered by monitoring agents in all of the nodes. A monitoring agent in the load generator collect statistics about dialogs to register the successfully executed dialogs (throughput), fraction of failed dialogs, and the dialog response time (DRT). These are the *service end-user metrics* considered in this service example.

In the cluster nodes performance measurements of cluster resource metrics like CPU, memory and network interfaces are needed for an understanding of the cluster-internal performance-relevant procedures. Existing tools can readily deliver such measurements like *ps, top* and *mpstat*. However, these tools are designed to provide instant and user friendly system statistics and are as such not very efficient. Instead dedicated node monitoring agents have been developed. En each cluster node they collect statistics from the /proc/ file system of Linux. This is basically a collection of file pointers to memory areas where the OS kernel provides direct access to kernel performance counters. Consequently they can be read with low resource overhead which has also been demonstrated in [10] and [15]. As previously emphasized, samples are not parsed but just stored directly in memory for later processing.

The node monitoring agents can be set to different sampling rates. For the experimental system considered in Sect. 5, at sampling rates of 100 Hz the node monitoring agent consumes on average less than 0.5 % CPU making them sufficient for this purpose.

4 Analytic Response Time Models

As dialogs from different concurrent calls may overlap at the cluster-based SIP-like call control server, they compete for the same processing and communication resources, hence an approach based on queueing models appears intuitively worthwhile. Furthermore, the cluster system also uses actual physical queues internally. In this section, *a basic* queueing model, a *load-dependent* extension, and a *tandem queueing model* are considered for extrapolation analysis.

4.1 Basic Queueing Model

The basic queueing model is presented in Fig. 5 and consists of a deterministic *delay stage* (M/D/∞ queue) followed by an *M/M/1/K queueing system*, hence it requires three parameters for its calibration: the duration of the deterministic delay, C_d, the exponential service rate, μ, and the buffer size K. The rational to introduce the deterministic delay stage is to allow to introduce a lower-bound on the transaction response times. With this model, the entire cluster is seen as a black-box without considering its multiple processes and multi-processing capabilities. The queueing system works on the level of transactions whereas client-centric performance metrics are defined at a dialog level. The exponential assumptions in the finite M/M/1/K queue are approximately correct for the arrival process of the call-control example in scenarios of higher load, namely with many overlapping dialogs; note that the dialog arrival rate is assumed to be Poisson, but the individual four transactions within a dialog are actually deterministically spaced (here with zero spacing in between). In order to include the sequence of dependent transactions within a dialog in the model, the mapping from dialog processing to transaction processing could be performed by introducing a feedback from the output of the M/M/1/K queue, as shown dotted in Fig. 5. However, as we are interested in high-load scenarios with many overlapping dialogs, this feedback is not considered, but instead the model input is on a transaction basis, where $\lambda = 4\Lambda$.

Note that this model basically models transactions. This is in line with the implementation of the simple SIP-like end-user service, which does not block access to the service at a dialog level but at the transaction level due to the finite queue. Thus the model correctly captures this aspect. However, a real end-user service implementation would be expected to block at the dialog level when resources become sparse, making this basic model insufficient.

The assumption of exponential service times in the M/M/1/K stage will be revisited later.

Closed-form expressions for the mean system time $E[S]$ for the M/M/1/K model can be found in any standard queueing theory book:

$$E[S]_{mm1k} = \frac{E[X]}{\lambda(1 - P_B)} = \frac{\rho + \rho^{K+1}(K\rho - K - 1)}{\lambda(1 - \rho^K)(1 - \rho)}, \quad \rho = \frac{\lambda}{\mu} . \tag{1}$$

$E[X]$ is the mean queue length an P_B is the blocking probability. As the model above works on transaction level, the mean dialog response time results as $DRT_{mean} = 4(E[S]_{mm1k} + C_d)$.

Parametrization of Model: Three different approaches have been studied for the parametrization of the basic model using basic measurements from the measurement platform. *(1) Black-box (BB) measurements* are only based on client metrics. The system is considered in a low load situation (here at 1.1 *dialogs/s*), where the probability of queueing is low. The parameters of the delay stage C_d then results as the minimum of the measured transaction response times. The mean service time $\bar{x}$ of the M/M/1/K system is then the estimated mean of the

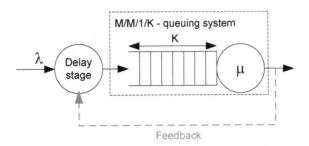

Fig. 5. A basic M/M/1/K queueing model with an additional delay stage

transaction response times shifted by their minimum. K, however, is not easily obtainable from measurements, and not at all obtainable from low-load measurements. Hence, it is calculated from knowledge of configured queue lengths of the incoming message queue in the cluster (which was identified via empirical experiments to be the bottleneck in the current service example on the used cluster implementation): The queue length is 400 KB, and an individual request consumes 500 B, hence $K \approx 800$.

To potentially provide a better estimate of $\bar{x}$, *(2) White-box (WB) measurements* are employed as the second calibration approach. They are based on cluster internal delay measurements of single transactions. The measurements are made in a *medium load* situation where the cluster is loaded approximately 50%. Reasons for this choice will be provided when discussing load-dependence aspects.

As a third method, a *(3) Least-Square (LS)* approach based on the resulting dialog response times is used to fit $\bar{x}$ and C_d. This parameter estimation approach is not targeted at extrapolation as it requires many individual measurements. However it enables a best case comparison of the model capabilities in relation to measurements.

4.2   Load-Dependent Model

Figure 6 depicts the empirical job time distributions as obtained by cluster-internal white-box measurements for the four different transactions in a dialog. Only Transaction 1 (dotted) is significantly different. In addition to context access it also includes the request to the location database in the call control server. The distributions are shown for low load and high load, where the job times are generally shorter in high-load scenarios. A likely explanation for this behavior is the superscalar architecture of the processors and the typically increasing efficiency of caching mechanisms for highly repetitive code execution. Similar results have been considered in [16].

In order to mimic the experimentally observed load dependence in a simplified manner in the queueing model, a threshold based service rate adjustment is included in the M/M/1/K model, making the service rate queue-length dependent:

$$\mu(n) = \begin{cases} \mu_1 \text{ for } n < Q \\ \mu_2 \text{ for } n \geq Q \end{cases} . \tag{2}$$

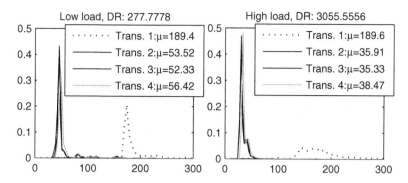

Fig. 6. The job time distribution of processing a request

Parametrization of the Load-dependent Model: In this case, the WB approach is needed for parametrization. μ_1 is still defined from job-time measurements at medium load where μ_2 is measured at high load to improve results when queueing (and for the model an accurate service time) has a significant impact on mean system time.

The threshold Q is chosen heuristically at $Q = 10$.

4.3   Extended Tandem Queueing Model

The basic models are limited in relation to considering a broad range of configuration options. Further they do not provide insight into the interaction between HA cluster services, HA end-user services and their consumption of system resources. These restrictions limit the kind of analysis than can be conducted. Consequently this is a motivation to consider extending the basic queueing model into a queueing network.

A very simple example is presented in Fig. 7. In this case the delay stage has been split into networking nodes and dispatcher processes. Dispatcher processes and the SIP-like service process are defined as $M/M/1$ queueing systems. This exemplifies how processes potentially could be modelled. The particular queueing network is called a *tandem queueing network* as there is only one route for the jobs to follow.

The mean transaction time then follows as $E[S_{total}] = E[S_{dpi}] + E[S_{sip}] + E[S_{dpo}] + 2E[S_{nw}]$. The individual expected values are approximated by assuming product form and Poisson arrivals in each stage.

Parametrization of Model: As a drawback of the increased power-fullness of the model, the number of parameters is increased: each queueing system in the queueing model needs to be parametrized individually via white-box measurements. Service times for the SIP-like service have already been discussed in the previous sections. Mean delays from the network can be estimated by round-trip time measurements. In this work job-time distribution measurements of the dispatcher have not been available. Instead a very rough approximation of its mean

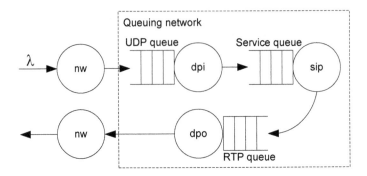

Fig. 7. Tandem queueing network

service time (assuming $E[S_{dpi}] = E[S_{dpo}]$) can been derived, from residual mean service times in a low load situation, when knowing the other mean service times in the system. This estimator also includes other delays caused e.g. by the load generator.

5   Measurements and Model Results

With the implemented measurement platform and a model basis, specific measurement scenarios can be conducted and the analytic modelling approaches can be validated.

5.1   Measurement-Based Results

The RTP HA cluster environment, used for measurements, is specified in Table 1 and its deployment is depicted in Fig. 8. It consists of a 2-node setup with a primary and a secondary backup node. In the subsequent results we consider a test-scenario studying varying context replication methods. Context Management is handled by a master process at the primary node and a backup process on the secondary. The replication method defines how context is copied to the secondary node. While more options exist, only *synchronous*, *asynchronous* and *no replication* configuration options are considered in this section. In the *asyn. replication* configuration the end-user service stores the context without verifying that it has been replicated correctly before continuing. In case of *syn. replication* the end-user service process is blocked until replication completes. This allows for error handling in case the replication fails. With *no replication* only the master process is active and no copying is conducted.

For extrapolation analysis mainly the end-user metrics have been studied in this work. Consequently only these results are presented here.

In the presented test-scenario a test-case is conducted for each setting of the context replication mode. For each test-case a set of test-runs are conducted each defining a specific load scenario. For these initial results each test-run has

Table 1. Basic cluster hardware and software configuration

Cluster configuration	
Size	One primary and one secondary node.
Processor and Memory	2-way Intel Xeon class server nodes, 6.256 GB
Interconnects	1 Gigabit Ethernet
Public network	1 Gigabit Ethernet
OS	Linux, SLES 9.0 - Kernel 2.6
Software	Fujitsu Siemens RTP V2.1A00 and PRIMECLUSTER V4.2A00

been conducted for 30 seconds where the first 5 seconds are a warm-up interval not used in the results. In a majority of the test runs, steady state of the load generation, resource consumption metrics and client metrics is reached within a few seconds.

Figure 9 depicts a measurement output of end-user metrics under different configurations of the context replication mode. The left graph depicts the measured mean DRT as the generated dialog rate increases. The mean response time is low until the system utilization gets nearer to 1, where it rapidly grows but then levels out due to the finiteness of input queues.

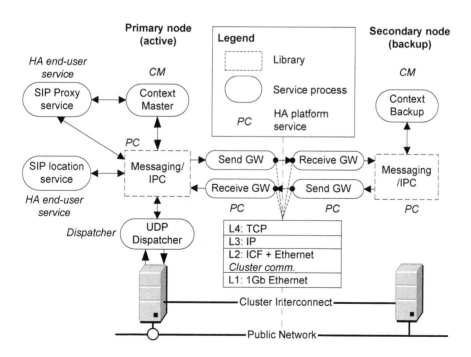

Fig. 8. The deployment of the SIP-like service in the HA cluster

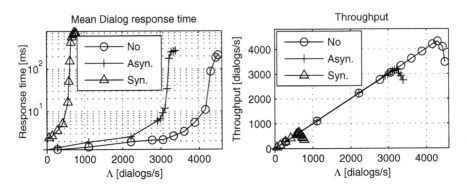

Fig. 9. Measured end-user client results at no, asynchronous and synchronous replication

The effect of high utilization is seen in the right half of Fig. 9 depicting the throughput. When requests are dropped, the transaction is timed out at the client, causing the entire dialog to be dropped. In this case this leads to a decreasing throughput as the generated dialog rate is increased.

Clearly no replication presents the best case in terms of performance. Asynchronous replication uses more resources for the message based reliable communication which increases service times and consequently causing a drop in the amount of clients which can be handled. Under synchronous replication the service is blocked while the primary node communicates with the secondary node. This becomes a bottleneck and clearly motivates for a parallelization of the service to process other transactions concurrently.

These measurement results can now be compared to extrapolation analysis conducted in the queueing models.

5.2   Basic Model

The basic model has been parametrized as described in Sect. 4. The parameters are listed in Table 2.

Table 2. Parameters of the M/M/1/K queue

	Black-box	White-box	LS-est.
Mean service time $\bar{x}$	58.25 μs	78.90 μs	78.18 μs
Queue length K	800 slots	800 slots	850 slots
Delay stage C_d	260 μs	260 μs	375 μs

The calculated DRT of different parametrization methods is presented in Fig. 10 in relation to measurements. The legend also specifies a *relative error*, which is the relative deviation of the analytic model from the measurement result averaged over the 13 measurement points.

Starting with the LS-estimated parameters, a good match between the measurement points and the graph from the analytic model can be observed. Actually at $\rho = 1$ the model predicts a maximum throughput of 3198 *dialogs/s* which matches the measurements. Thus the model type, a constant delay stage in sequence with an M/M/1/K queue, seems principally capable of representing the main characteristics of the considered cluster implementation of the call control service.

Moving on to the black-box results there is a clear underestimation of DRT in all cases. Comparing to the LS-estimated parameters of $\bar{x}$ it is approximately 20 μs lower in case of the black-box model (Table 2). A large part of this deviation may be caused by the approach to attribute the minimum observed delays completely to the deterministic delay stage, at which no queueing occurs. Another potential inaccuracy is the assumption of exponentially distributed dialog transaction times, which in fact show higher variance in their empirical distribution.

The calibration problem of determining the delay contributions of the constant delay stage, does not occur with white-box measurements. The white-box measurements are in this case close to the LS-estimated parameters, providing a much better extrapolation result. Thus white-box measurements have been used throughout the further extrapolation analysis cases in this paper.

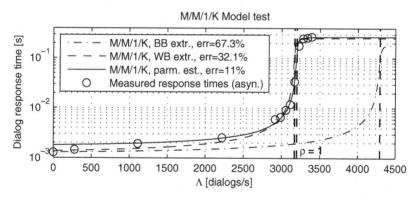

Fig. 10. M/M/1/K, extrapolated and parameter estimated results in relation to measurements

The queue size K has been determined from the RTP configuration settings to a slightly lower value than in the parameter estimate. Possibly there could be an inconsistency between actual RTP queue length and the configured. There could also be unmodelled handling of message buffer overflow i.e. retries or other unconsidered delays, in the load generator and the cluster system, during overload situations.

When looking at the delay stage, there is a significant difference between the parameters extracted from simple measurements and the parameter estimation approach. The LS-estimate is dominated by a majority of measurements at high load, where also the errors to minimize are most significant. As a result the first two measurements in the data set have a small significance. However the measurements in low load situations are important for the other extrapolation approaches. Consequently the cause of the difference between estimates and extrapolated results are of interest. A part of the explanation could be the previously presented gain from processing optimizations. As load increases some of the queueing effect is eliminated by faster job times causing deviation from the model in low load situations. Clearly, also other processes in the HA platform, not considered by this model, can have an influence; i.e. the UDP dispatcher and/or messaging services.

5.3   Load-Dependent Queueing Model

In Fig. 11 the DRT results from the load-dependent model are presented considering the *no replication* case and an M/M/1 model with WB parameters (job-times measured at high load). Now two parameters exist to describe the load at medium and high load. The model exerts a higher mean DRT at lower loads in relation to the M/M/1 model while at high loads it corresponds to the M/M/1 model. In relation to the visual measurement points and the relative error the load dependent model seems slightly better. These results do not prove that load dependencies can describe most of the deviations between the basic model and measurements. However, the load dependency-effects clearly appear, making this model variant relevant in future improvements of the modelling method.

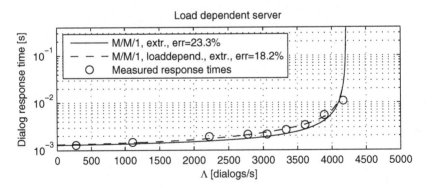

Fig. 11. DRT at no replication with a load dependent model

5.4   Extended Tandem Queueing Model

Finally Fig. 12 considers measurement results from the extended model. Not surprisingly the outcome is very close to what the basic queueing model produced. Clearly the most significant influence on the output comes from the processing in the SIP HA end-user service, i.e. in the considered service and deployment example, the bottleneck is the SIP process.

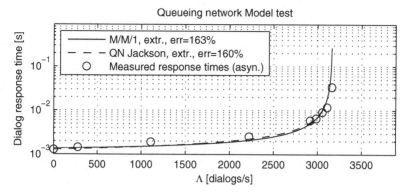

Fig. 12. Queueing model, extrapolated results in relation to measurements and an M/M/1 model

A very rough approximation of the dispatcher mean service time has been made. In reality neither its service time distribution nor mean service time is known. This provides reasonable results for the analysis of mean system times but could potentially cause faulty results in other metrics to consider e.g. resource consumption or dialog response time distributions.

To use the basic queueing model, in establishing the performance impact of overhead from different configuration options, an assessment of the mean service time for each configuration is needed. This has successfully been done for each of the considered cases in Fig. 9. However, it requires reconfiguration efforts for each configuration to study. As opposed to the basic model the considered queuing network allows a specification of the processes in the HA cluster system. This could potentially be used to consider different configuration options related to the processes and their interaction. For instance the timely overhead from a synchronous call between cluster nodes could be established and possibly allow extrapolation from the asyn. replication to syn replication without additional measurements. It is also expected that the queueing network model can handle cases for analysis where the basic model is not sufficient. I.e. when jobs from transactions are routed to different processes in the the system e.g. in load balancing cases. This should be studied further in future work with more complex HA end-user services and configurations considering multiple job classes. In addition the secondary node should be included in the model to consider its configuration options.

Clearly it is also of interest to include more performance variables than mean DRT. Assuming these basic models are sufficient, other end-user metrics may easily be derived from state probabilities. E.g computation of tail probabilities can be used to define how long users could *risk* waiting for service. Potentially the queueing models can also be used to calculate steady state performance metrics for utilization of CPU, network and disk drives [17].

6   Summary and Outlook

Due to the expected future increase of communicating end-user services that benefit from High-Availability (and reliability), the interest in generically applicable mechanisms and tools to account for fault-tolerance in the deployed service is expected to rise accordingly; one major candidate that simplifies the development and deployment of such HA services are cluster solutions with supporting HA middleware, which provide functionalities such as process management and reliable inter-process communication, reliable data storage and access transparently to end-user clients and to some extend also to network operators. As the price for the increased availability and reliability are increased costs due to additional Hardware and Software as well as increased run-time overhead due to additional communication and processing in the cluster middleware, it is of particular importance, to be able to quantify the impact of certain cluster configurations on performance as perceived by the end-users.

This paper has introduced a performance evaluation approach which uses both measurement-based analysis under emulated client load patterns as well as simple analytic queueing models to characterize the end-user performance behaviour. The approach is applied to the example of an abstracted SIP-like call control service, for which simple analytic queueing models based on $M/M/1/K$ queues fed by constant delay stages show a remarkable good prediction of response time with only very limited calibration effort. Further improvements results, if load-dependence properties and non-exponential service times are taken into account, which can be achieved with only introducing few additional model parameters that are easy to calibrate.

As the call control service has some rather simple structure, although not uncommon in reality, more complex service patterns may also lead to more complex analytic models, in particular of specific insights into the impact of different functionalities of the HA middleware need to be obtained. An approach for such scenarios has been outlined in Sect. 5.4 using tandem or more complex queue models, for which the computational effort for calculations of response times however is rather strongly dependent on details of the model, in particular the applicability of exponential assumptions. The application of the analysis approach to more complex service types is however left for future work. Also, the paper only presents a selected subset of the available measurement results; more detailed case studies applying the introduced approach and based on the described tools will be presented in the future.

References

1. Service Availability Forum: Service Availability Forum - Application Interface Specification. (November 2004)
2. Kim, P., Boehm, W.: Support for real-time applications in future mobile networks: the ims approach. In: Proceedings of WPMC 03. (October 2003)
3. Neuts, M.: Matrix-geometric solutions in stochastic models. John Hopkins University Press (1981)

4. Lipsky, L.: Queueing theory: A linear algebraic approach. MacMillian Publishing Company, New York (1992)
5. Fujitsu Siemens Computers: SAForum Implementation Guide. (April 2006)
6. GoAhead: SelfReliant Technical Product Description. (September 2005)
7. Guinn, K., Padghan, S.: Achieving high availability in linux-based cluster environments. Dell Power Solutions (August 2006)
8. Sun Microsystems: Sun Cluster Overview for Solaris OS. (September 2004)
9. Rosenberg, J., Schulzrinne, H., Camarillo, G., Johnston, A., Peterson, J., Sparks, R., Handley, M., Schooler, E.: SIP: Session Initiation Protocol, RFC3261. Network Working Group. (Hune 2002)
10. Sottile, M.J., Minnich, R.G.: Supermon: A high-speed cluster monitoring system. In: CLUSTER '02: Proceedings of the IEEE International Conference on Cluster Computing, Washington, DC, USA, IEEE Computer Society (2002) 39—46
11. Skoog, P., Arnold, D.: Nanosecond-level precision timing comes to military applications. COTS Journal **7** (2005)
12. Mosberger, D., Jin, T.: httperf: A tool for measuring web server performance. In: First Workshop on Internet Server Performance, ACM (June 1998) 59—67
13. Grønbæk, J.: Model based performance analysis of an ha cluster. Technical report, Department of Electronic Systems, Aalborg University (2007)
14. Jamjoom, H., Shin, K.: Eve: A scalable network client emulator (2003) Eve: A Scalable Network Client Emulator, University of Michigan Technical Report, Tech. Rep. CSE-TR-478-03, 2003.
15. Smith, C., Henry, D.: High-performance linux cluster monitoring using java. In: Proceedings of the 3rd Linux Cluster International Conference. (2002)
16. Engblom, J.: Analysis of the execution time unpredictability caused by dynamic branch prediction. In: IEEE Real Time Technology and Applications Symposium. (2003) 152–159
17. Jenq, B.C., Kohler, W.H., Towsley, D.: A queueing network model for a distributed database testbed system. IEEE Trans. Softw. Eng. **14**(7) (1988) 908–921

A Faster Estimation Algorithm for Periodic Preventive Rejuvenation Schedule Maximizing System Availability

Koichiro Rinsaka[1] and Tadashi Dohi[2]

[1] Department of Business Administration, Kobe Gakuin University
Kobe 650–8586, Japan
[2] Department of Information Engineering, Hiroshima University
Higashi-Hiroshima 739–8527, Japan
dohi@rel.hiroshima-u.ac.jp

Abstract. It is of great importance to perform preventive rejuvenation of software systems with service degradation. In this paper we develop a faster estimation algorithm for the optimal periodic rejuvenation schedule which maximizes the steady-state system availability. In the case with unknown system failure time distribution, a non-parametric estimation approach based on the empirical distribution of system failure time has been proposed in the literature, but often failed to obtain the exact estimates for the small sample cases. We improve the existing availability estimation algorithm in terms of convergence speed and derive the more effective estimation scheme based on the kernel density of system failure time. Throughout simulation experiments, the proposed estimation scheme is compared with the existing approach and can be validated in the sense of asymptotic optimality.

Keywords: system availability, software aging, preventive maintenance, periodic rejuvenation, non-parametric statistics, kernel density estimation.

1   Introduction

When many software systems around us are executed continuously for long periods of time, some of the faults cause them to age due to the error conditions that accrue with time and/or load. Especially, *the aging-related bugs*, which are due to the phenomenon of resource exhaustion, may exist in operating systems, middleware and application software. For instance, operating system resources such as swap space and free memory available are progressively depleted due to defects in software such as memory leaks and incomplete cleanup of resources after use. It is well known that *software aging* will affect the performance of applications and eventually cause them to fail [1], [2], [7], [15], [25], [32]. Software aging has been observed in widely-used communication software like Internet Explorer, Netscape and xrn as well as commercial operating systems and middleware.

M. Malek et al.(Eds.): ISAS 2007, LNCS 4526, pp. 94–109, 2007.
© Springer-Verlag Berlin Heidelberg 2007

A complementary approach to handle software aging and its related transient failures, called *software rejuvenation*, has already become popular [17] as a typical and low cost environment diversity technique of operational software. Software rejuvenation is a preventive and proactive solution that is particularly useful for counteracting the phenomenon of software aging. It involves stopping the running software occasionally, cleaning its internal state and restarting it. Cleaning the internal state of a software might involve garbage collection, flushing operating system kernel tables, reinitializing internal data structures and hardware reboot. In general, two approaches: measurement-based approach and modeling-based approach, are taken to study the software dependability caused by aging-related bugs. The former mainly focuses on the detection/identification of software aging phenomena, and explains them physically in real applications [1], [2], [7], [15], [25]. On the other hand, the latter corresponds to both design and environment diversity techniques and their quantitative evaluation.

Huang *et al.* [17] represented a degradation phenomenon of telecommunication billing application by a two-step failure model. From the clean state the software system jumps into a degraded state from which two actions are possible: rejuvenation with return to the clean state or transition to the system failure state. They modeled a four-state process by a continuous-time Markov chain (CTMC) and derived the steady-state system availability and the expected operation cost per unit time in the steady state. Dohi *et al.* [9], [10] extended the Huang *et al.*'s CTMC model [17] to the continuous and discrete-time semi-Markov processes (SMPs). Rinsaka and Dohi [24] analyzed the stochastic behavior of fault-tolerant software systems in order to investigate both effects of redundancy and preventive rejuvenation. Tai *et al.* [28] presented an approach on on-board preventive maintenance which rejuvenates a mission critical system by letting the system components rotate, and successfully enhanced the mission reliability.

As another examples, the effects of aging as crash/hang failure, referred to as *hard failure*, and of aging as *soft failure* that can lead to performance degradation, are actually observed in many applications. Pfening *et al.* [21] modeled a performance degradation process by the gradual decrease of processing rate in a non-stationary Markovian queueing system, and formulated a determination problem of the optimal preventive rejuvenation schedule by a Markov decision process. Eto and Dohi [12] analyzed a non-queueing model with multistage service degradation levels and characterized the optimal preventive rejuvenation policy via a semi-Markov decision process. Garg *et al.* [14] considered a transaction-based software system, which involves arrival and queueing of jobs, and analyzed both effects of aging; hard failures that result in an unavailability and soft failures that result in performance degradation.

Bobbio *et al.* [6] formulated workload-based rejuvenation scheduling problems with a cumulative damage model. Since the system workload is deeply related to the software aging phenomena, the workload-based analysis of aging and rejuvenation may be significant to implement the preventive maintenance of operational software systems. Bao *et al.* [4], [5] proposed an adaptive preventive rejuvenation scheme and estimated the rejuvenation timing with the real aging data. Wang *et al.* [31] further presented the performability analysis of clustered systems with rejuvenation under varying workload. Vaidyanathan and Trivedi [29] developed a comprehensive approach to bridge the gap between the measurement-based approach and the analytical modeling approach, named measurement-based semi-Markov workload model. Avritzer *et al.* [3] also proposed three algorithms for detecting the need for preventive rejuvenation by monitoring the changing values of a customer-effecting performance metric such as response time. The underlying model there is a multiserver Markovian queue and the resulting algorithms are based on simple parametric statistics. Reinecke *et al.* [22] and van Moorsel and Wolter [30] considered interesting restart policies as an application-level rejuvenation technique, and derived the computation algorithms to minimize higher moments of job completion time. They also considered on-line algorithms based on the time series analysis technique with auto correlation for determining the application level restart time. Recently, an nice practice guide to the resource forecasting for the Apache web server was provided by Hoffmann *et al.* [16]. They summarized the experimental approach and statistical analysis as well as the modeling technique.

In this paper we consider again a basic two-step failure model considered by the seminal contributions in [9], [17] among several modeling techniques. Garg *et al.* [13] introduced the idea of periodic rejuvenation (deterministic interval between successive rejuvenations) into the Huang *et al.*'s model [17] and represented the stochastic behavior by using a Markov regenerative stochastic Petri net. Suzuki *et al.* [27] and Iwamoto *et al.* [18] extended the Garg *et al.*'s model [13] to the continuous and discrete-time SMPs. Similar to the works in [9], [10], they developed statistically non-parametric algorithms to estimate the optimal preventive rejuvenation schedule from the complete samples of system failure time data without censoring. The fundamental idea in [9], [10], [18], [27] was to represent the steady-state system availability as a function of the empirical distribution on system failure time. In other words, since their estimation algorithms are statistically *consistent*, the resulting estimators approach to the real (but unknown) optimal solutions asymptotically, even if one does not specify the system failure time distributions. This property is very powerful to implement the rejuvenation protocol under uncertain usage environment of operational software.

However, it is worth mentioning that the estimators of the optimal preventive rejuvenation schedule mentioned above are based on an implicit assumption of *large sample* on system failure time, and that they can be validated only for the case with a sufficient number of system failure data. In other words, for an operational software system with higher availability requirement, since we seldom encounter the frequent system failures in operational phase, it would be impossible to get the exact estimates by using the empirical distribution for the small sample cases. In this paper we develop a faster estimation algorithm for the optimal periodic rejuvenation schedule which maximizes the steady-state system availability. We improve the existing availability estimation algorithm in terms of convergence speed and derive the more effective estimation scheme based on the kernel density of system failure time. Throughout simulation experiments, the proposed estimation scheme is compared with the existing approach and can be validated in the sense of asymptotic optimality. The results are really applicable to implement an on-line rejuvenation protocol in the case with unknown failure time distribution, and will be useful for the software end users in the operational phase.

2   Two-Step Failure Model with Periodic Rejuvenation

2.1   Model Description

Consider the similar stochastic model with periodic software rejuvenation to Garg *et al.* [13] and Suzuki *et al.* [27] in continuous time. Suppose that the operation of a software system starts at time $t = 0$ in the highly robust state (normal operation state). Let Z_0 be the random time interval when the highly robust state changes to the failure-probable state, having the common continuous probability distribution function $\Pr\{Z_0 \leq t\} = F_0(t)$ with finite mean μ_0 (> 0). Let X denote the transition time from the failure-probable state to the system failure state, which is the non-negative random variable having the continuous probability distribution function $\Pr\{X \leq t\} = F_f(t)$ with finite mean μ_f (> 0). The preventive rejuvenation is performed at a pre-scheduled time which is measured from the start (or restart) of software operation in the robust state. The continuous probability distribution function of the time to invoke preventive rejuvenation is at the moment given by $F_r(t)$ with finite mean t_0 (≥ 0). In this case the time to complete preventive rejuvenation is also the non-negative random variable having the continuous probability distribution function $F_c(t)$ with finite mean μ_c (> 0). After completing the preventive rejuvenation, the software system can become as good as new at the beginning of the next highly robust state. On the other hand, if the system failure occurs before triggering preventive rejuvenation, then the recovery operation starts immediately, where

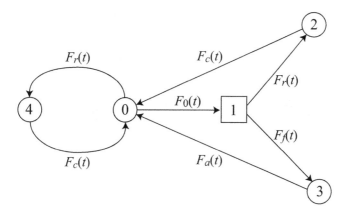

Fig. 1. Transition diagram of Markov regenerative process

the time to complete the recovery, Y, is the non-negative random variable having the continuous probability distribution function $\Pr\{Y \leq t\} = F_a(t)$ with finite mean $\mu_a \ (> 0)$. After completing the recovery operation, the software system can become as good as new. The same cycle from the start/restart of software operation to the next start/restart repeats again and again over an infinite time horizon.

To analyze the stochastic behavior of underlying periodic software rejuvenation model, we introduce the Markov regenerative process [13], [27]. Figure 1 illustrates the transition diagram of the stochastic model under consideration, where

State 0: highly robust state (normal operation state)
State 1: failure probable state
State 2: preventive rejuvenation state from failure probable state
State 3: system failure state
State 4: preventive rejuvenation state from highly robust state.

In the figure the states denoted by circles (0, 2, 3, 4) and square (1) are regeneration and non-regeneration points, respectively. Since this stochastic process involves only one non-regeneration point, it is relatively easy to transform the underlying Markov regenerative process to a semi-Markov process. Before doing this, suppose that the time to invoke the preventive rejuvenation is given by a constant t_0 without any loss of generality. This is because the preventive rejuvenation should be scheduled for the pre-scheduled constant interval in practice [13], [27], so that

$$F_r(t) = U(t - t_0) = \begin{cases} 1 & \text{for } t \geq t_0 \\ 0 & \text{otherwise} \end{cases} \tag{1}$$

where $U(\cdot)$ is the unit step function. We call $t_0 \ (\geq 0)$ *the preventive (periodic) rejuvenation schedule* in this paper.

2.2 Semi-markov Analysis

We analytically derive the steady-state system availability. Since five states: State 0 ∼ State 4 in Fig. 1 are reduced to three states; normal state (**State N**), system failure state (**State F**) and preventive rejuvenation state (**State R**), we have the equivalent semi-Markov process to the Markov regenerative process. Define $G(t) = (F_0 * F_f)(t)$, where '$*$' denotes the Stieltjes convolution, *i.e.*,

$$(A * B)(t) = \int_0^t A(t - x) dB(x) \tag{2}$$

for two continuous functions $A(t)$ and $B(t)$ with positive support. Figure 2 depicts the equivalent semi-Markov transition diagram to Fig. 1. We call the

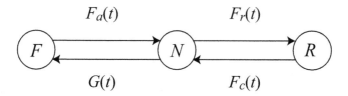

Fig. 2. Transition diagram of semi-Markov process

probability distribution $G(t)$ *system failure time distribution.* From the standard argument of semi-Markov process, let $P_{i,j}(t)$, $i,j = N, F, R$, be the transition probability that the system makes transition from State i to State j at time t. Then, we have

$$P_{N,N}(t) = \int_0^t \overline{F_r}(x)d(G * P_{F,N})(x) + \int_0^t \overline{G}(x)d(F_r * P_{R,N})(x) + \overline{G}(t) \cdot \overline{F_r}(t),$$
$$(3)$$

$$P_{N,F}(t) = \int_0^t \overline{F_r}(x)d(G * P_{F,F})(x) + \int_0^t \overline{G}(x)d(F_r * P_{R,F})(x), \tag{4}$$

$$P_{N,R}(t) = \int_0^t \overline{F_r}(x)d(G * P_{F,R})(x) + \int_0^t \overline{G}(x)d(F_r * P_{R,R})(x), \tag{5}$$

$$P_{F,N}(t) = (F_a * P_{N,N})(t), \tag{6}$$

$$P_{F,F}(t) = \overline{F_a}(t) + (F_a * P_{N,F})(t), \tag{7}$$

$$P_{F,R}(t) = (F_a * P_{N,R})(t), \tag{8}$$

$$P_{R,F}(t) = (F_c * P_{N,F})(t), \tag{9}$$

$$P_{R,N}(t) = (F_c * P_{N,N})(t), \tag{10}$$

$$P_{R,R}(t) = \overline{F_c}(t) + (F_c * P_{N,R})(t), \tag{11}$$

where in general $\phi(\cdot) = 1 - \phi(\cdot)$.

Theorem 1. *For an arbitrary $i = N, F, R$, the steady-state system availability $AV(t_0)$ as a function of t_0 is given by*

$$AV(t_0) = \lim_{t \to \infty} P_{i,N}(t) = S(t_0)/T(t_0), \tag{12}$$

where

$$S(t_0) = \int_0^{t_0} \overline{G}(t)dt, \tag{13}$$

$$T(t_0) = \int_0^{t_0} \overline{G}(t)dt + \mu_a G(t_0) + \mu_c \overline{G}(t_0). \tag{14}$$

3   Statistical Estimation Algorithms

3.1   Optimal Preventive Rejuvenation

In Section 2, we obtained the steady-state system availability $AV(t_0)$. Of our next concern is to seek the optimal preventive rejuvenation schedule t_0^* which maximizes the system availability $AV(t_0)$. We make the following parametric assumption:

(A-1) $\mu_a > \mu_c$.

The assumption (A-1) means that the mean time to complete the recovery operation is strictly larger than the mean time to complete the preventive rejuvenation. This assumption is intuitively reasonable to motivate triggering the preventive rejuvenation in terms of maximizing system availability. The following result characterizes the optimal preventive rejuvenation schedule.

Theorem 2. *(1) Suppose that the system failure time distribution $G(t) = (F_0 * F_f)(t)$ is strictly IFR (increasing failure rate) under the assumption (A-1), i.e., the corresponding hazard rate*

$$r(t_0) = \frac{\int_0^{t_0} f_f(t_0 - x)\, dF_0(x)}{\overline{G}(t_0)} \tag{15}$$

is strictly increasing in t_0, where $f_f(x) = dF_f(x)/dx$. Define the following non-linear function:

$$q(t_0) = T(t_0) - \left\{ (\mu_a - \mu_c)r(t_0) + 1 \right\} S(t_0). \tag{16}$$

(i) *If $q(\infty) < 0$, then there exists a finite and unique optimal preventive rejuvenation schedule t_0^* $(0 < t_0^* < \infty)$ satisfying $q(t_0^*) = 0$, and the maximum steady-state system availability is given by*

$$AV(t_0^*) = \frac{1}{(\mu_a - \mu_c)r(t_0^*) + 1}. \tag{17}$$

(ii) *If $q(\infty) \geq 0$, then the optimal preventive rejuvenation schedule is $t_0^* \to \infty$, i.e., it is optimal not to perform the preventive rejuvenation. Then the steady-state system availability becomes*

$$AV(\infty) = \frac{\mu_0 + \lambda_f}{\mu_0 + \lambda_f + \mu_a}. \tag{18}$$

(2) Suppose that the system failure time distribution $G(t)$ is DFR (decreasing failure rate) under the assumption (A-1), i.e., $r(t_0)$ is decreasing in t_0. Then, the steady-state system availability $AV(t_0)$ is a quasi-convex function of t_0, and the optimal preventive rejuvenation schedule is given by $t_0^* \to \infty$.

From Theorem 2, if the parametric form of system failure time distribution function $G(t)$ is given, it is possible to derive the optimal preventive rejuvenation schedule analytically.

3.2 Non-parametric Estimation

Next, suppose that n observations; $0 = x_0 \leq x_1 \leq x_2 \leq \cdots \leq x_n$, sampled from an absolutely continuous system failure time distribution G, are available. Based on this fixed sample, we define the empirical distribution function:

$$G_n(t_0) = \begin{cases} j/n & \text{for } x_j \leq t_0 < x_{j+1}, \\ 1 & \text{for } x_n \leq t_0 \end{cases} \tag{19}$$

for $0 \leq t_0 < \infty$. Using the well-established technique in [9], [27], we define the total time on test statistics for the sample data x_j, $j = 0, 1, 2, \cdots, n$, by

$$\int_0^{t_0} \overline{G}_n(y)dy = \begin{cases} \sum_{k=1}^j (n - k + 1)(x_k - x_{k-1}), \\ \qquad \text{for } x_j \leq t_0 < x_{j+1}, \\ \sum_{k=1}^n (n - k + 1)(x_k - x_{k-1}), \\ \qquad \text{for } x_n \leq t_0. \end{cases} \tag{20}$$

From Eqs.(19) and (20), it can be seen that a non-parametric estimate of $AV(t_0)$ (empirical system availability) is given by

$$AV_n(t_0) = \frac{\sum_{k=1}^j (n - k + 1)(x_k - x_{k-1})}{\mu_a j/n + \mu_c(n-j)/n + \sum_{k=1}^j (n-k+1)(x_k - x_{k-1})} \tag{21}$$

for an arbitrary discrete point $t_0 = x_j$, $j = 0, 1, \cdots, n$. Because it is evident that for $t_0 \in (x_j, x_{j+1})$ $AV_n(t_0) \leq AV_n(x_j)$, the maximum system availability can be attained by any of data points x_j.

Theorem 3. *(i) A non-parametric estimate of the optimal preventive rejuvenation schedule which maximizes $AV(t_0)$ is given by $\hat{t}_0^* = x_{j^*}$, where*

$$j^* = \left\{ j \mid \max_{0 \leq j \leq n} \frac{n \sum_{k=1}^j (n - k + 1)(x_k - x_{k-1})}{[j/n + \mu_c/(\mu_a - \mu_c)] \sum_{k=1}^n x_k} \right\}. \tag{22}$$

(ii) The estimate given in (i) is strongly consistent, i.e., $\hat{t}_0^*$ converges to the optimal solution t_0^* uniformly with probability one as $n \to \infty$, if a unique optimal preventive rejuvenation schedule exists.

From Theorem 3, it is seen that the consistent estimate $\hat{t}_0^*$ with asymptotical optimality can be obtained from the complete sample of x_j without specifying the system failure time distribution G. However, as mentioned in Section 1, the resulting estimate is derived based on only the empirical distribution $G_n(t_0)$. This implies that a sufficient number of failure data are needed to get an exact estimate of the optimal preventive rejuvenation schedule.

4 Kernel Density Estimation

In order to refine the estimate given in Theorem 3 it would be useful to improve the convergence speed of the empirical distribution, *i.e.*, $G_n(t_0) \to G(t_0)$ and

Table 1. Typical kernel functions [26]

Kernel	$K(t)$
Rectangular	$\dfrac{1}{2}$ for $|t| < 1$, otherwise 0
Gaussian	$\dfrac{1}{\sqrt{2\pi}} e^{-(1/2)t^2}$
Triangular	$1 - |t|$ for $|t| < 1$, otherwise 0
Biweight	$\dfrac{15}{16}\left(1 - t^2\right)^2$ for $|t| < 1$, otherwise 0
Epanechnikov	$\dfrac{3}{4}\left(1 - \dfrac{1}{5}t^2\right)/\sqrt{5}$ for $|t| < \sqrt{5}$, otherwise 0

$\int_0^{t_0} \overline{G}_n(y)dy \to \int_0^{t_0} \overline{G}(y)dy$ for fixed t_0. In this section, we replace the empirical distribution in an estimate of the steady-state system availability in Eq.(21) by the kernel type empirical distribution. Suppose that the system failure time data $x_1, x_2, \cdots, x_n$ are the sample from the probability density function $f_0 * f_f$, where $f_0(t) = dF_0(t)/dt$. Define the kernel density estimator [8], [20], [23], [26] by

$$(f_0 * f_f)_{n,k}(t) = \frac{1}{nh} \sum_{i=1}^{n} K\left(\frac{t - x_i}{h}\right), \tag{23}$$

where h (> 0) is the window width called the *smoothing parameter* or *bandwidth*, and the function $K(\cdot)$ is called the *kernel function* which satisfies the following condition:

$$\int_{-\infty}^{\infty} K(t)dt = 1, \quad \int_{-\infty}^{\infty} tK(t)dt = 0, \quad 0 < \int_{-\infty}^{\infty} t^2 K(t)dt < \infty. \tag{24}$$

Usually, but not always, the function $K(\cdot)$ is selected as a symmetric probability density function. In Table 1, we summarize the typical kernel functions used in statistical inference [26]. In this paper, we apply the following Gaussian kernel function:

$$K(t) = \frac{1}{\sqrt{2\pi}} e^{-(1/2)t^2} \tag{25}$$

to estimate the density function of the system failure time, $(f_0 * f_f)(t)$. The main reason to use it is its tractability and convergence property. Based on the kernel estimator in Eq.(23), we define an estimate of $\int_0^{t_0} \overline{G}(y)dy$ by

$$KDE_n(t_0) = \int_0^{t_0} \left\{ 1 - (F_0 * F_f)_{n,k}(t) \right\} dt, \tag{26}$$

where $(F_0 * F_f)_{n,k}(t) = \int_0^t (f_0 * f_f)_{n,k}(y)dy$ in Eq.(23).

Theorem 4. *(i) A non-parametric kernel density estimate of the optimal pre-ventive rejuvenation schedule which maximizes $AV(t_0)$ is given by $\hat{t}_0^{**}$ which is the solution of the maximization problem:*

$$\max_{0 \le t_0 \le \infty} \frac{KDE_n(t_0)}{[(F_0 * F_f)_{n,k}(t_0) + \mu_c/(\mu_a - \mu_c)] \sum_{k=1}^{n} x_k/n}. \tag{27}$$

(ii) The estimate given in (i) is strongly consistent, i.e., $\hat{t}_0^{**}$ converges to the optimal solution t_0^* uniformly with probability one as $n \to \infty$, if a unique optimal preventive rejuvenation schedule exists.

From Theorem 4 it is easy to see that the estimate of the optimal periodic preventive rejuvenation schedule is obtained by calculating the optimal point t_0^{**} maximizing the tangent slope from the point $(-\mu_c/(\mu_a - \mu_c), \, 0)$ to the curve $(t_0, \, KDE_n(t_0))$ in the two-dimensional plane (see [9], [10], [18], [27]).

   When we utilize the kernel method mentioned above, the problem of choosing the design parameter h in Eq.(23) is of crucial importance. The most plausible way to select the bandwidth is to minimize the mean integrated squares error (MISE) [23]:

$$\text{MISE} = \text{E} \int_{-\infty}^{\infty} \left[(f_0 * f_f)_{n,k}(x) - (f_0 * f_f)(x) \right]^2 dx. \tag{28}$$

Further, we obtain the following approximate form:

$$\begin{aligned}
\text{MISE} &= \int_{-\infty}^{\infty} \text{E} \left[(f_0 * f_f)_{n,k}(x) - (f_0 * f_f)(x) \right]^2 dx \\
&= \int_{-\infty}^{\infty} \left\{ \text{E} \left[(f_0 * f_f)_{n,k}(x) \right] - (f_0 * f_f)(x) \right\}^2 dx \\
&\quad + \int_{-\infty}^{\infty} \text{Var} \left[(f_0 * f_f)_{n,k}(x) \right] dx \\
&\approx \frac{1}{4} h^4 r^2 \int_{-\infty}^{\infty} (f_0 * f_f)_{n,k}''(x)^2 dx + n^{-1} h^{-1} \int_{-\infty}^{\infty} K(t)^2 dt, \tag{29}
\end{aligned}$$

where "''" denotes the twice differentiation. It can be shown that the best band-width in terms of minimization of Eq.(29) is given by [20]

$$h_{ideal} = r^{-2/5} \left\{ \int_{-\infty}^{\infty} K(t)^2 dt \right\}^{1/5} \left\{ \int_{-\infty}^{\infty} (f_0 * f_f)''(x)^2 dx \right\}^{-1/5} n^{-1/5}. \tag{30}$$

Under the assumption that the kernel function is given by the normal distribution with density φ and variance σ^2, it can be seen that

$$\int_{-\infty}^{\infty} (f_0 * f_f)_{n,k}''(x)^2 dx = \sigma^{-5} \int_{-\infty}^{\infty} \varphi''(x)^2 dx = \frac{3}{8} \varphi^{-1/2} \sigma^{-5}. \tag{31}$$

Finally, substituting the Gaussian kernel in Eq.(25) into Eq.(30) yields

$$h_{ideal} = (4\pi)^{-1/10} \frac{3}{8} \pi^{-1/2} \sigma n^{-1/5}$$

$$= \left(\frac{4}{3}\right)^{1/5} \sigma n^{-1/5} \approx 1.06 \sigma n^{-1/5}. \tag{32}$$

From Eq.(32) it is easily checked that the ideal bandwidth becomes small as the number of observed data increases.

5 Simulation Experiments

Of our next interest is the investigation of asymptotic properties and convergence speed of estimators proposed in this paper. Suppose that the random variables, Z_0 and X, obey the following exponential and the Weibull distributions:

$$F_0(t) = 1 - e^{-t/\mu_0}, \quad \mu_0 > 0, \tag{33}$$

$$F_f(t) = 1 - e^{-\left(\frac{t}{\theta}\right)^\gamma}, \quad \gamma > 0, \ \theta > 0, \tag{34}$$

respectively. It is assumed throughout the numerical examples that $\mu_0 = 240.00$, $\gamma = 2.00$, $\theta = 2400.00$, $\mu_a = 0.50$ and $\mu_c = 0.16$. In this situation, if we can know both the probability distributions $F_0(t)$ and $F_f(t)$ completely, then the optimal periodic preventive rejuvenation schedule and its associated maximum system availability can be calculated as $t_0^* = 1742.14$ (hr) and $A(t_0^*) = 0.999826$, respectively. First, let us consider the estimation of an optimal periodic preventive rejuvenation schedule maximizing the steady-state system availability when the system failure time data are already observed but the corresponding probability distribution is unknown. We generate 30 pseudo random numbers based on Eqs.(33) and (34) as the system failure time data. For the 30 pseudo random numbers, we determine the bandwidth as $h_{ideal} = 583.18$ from Eq.(32). Finally, we estimate the optimal periodic preventive rejuvenation schedule and its associated maximum system availability as $\hat{t}_0^{**} = 1982.33$ (hr) and $AV(\hat{t}_0^{**}) = 0.999850$, respectively.

Next, we investigate the asymptotic behavior of the proposed kernel density estimator and compare it with the existing non-parametric estimation approach based on the empirical distribution. To do it, the Monte Carlo simulations are carried out with pseudo random numbers based on the exponential and the Weibull distributions given in Eqs.(33) and (34). Figure 3 reveals the asymptotic behavior of the optimal preventive rejuvenation schedule. It is found that the both estimates converge to the real optimal solution when more than 40 data are available. In Fig. 4, we plot the convergence behavior of estimates of system availability. From this figure, 20 data are enough to estimate the accurate availability $A(t_0^*) = 0.999826$.

Finally, we examine the convergence speed and accuracy of the kernel method for the different failure time distribution. In Figs 5 through 10 we calculate the relative absolute error averages, $RAEA_{t_0}$ and $RAEA_{AV}$, of estimates of the optimal preventive rejuvenation schedule and maximum system availability, respectively where

$$RAEA_{t_0} = \frac{1}{mt_0^*} \sum_{j=1}^{m} \left| \hat{t}_{0_j}^{**} - t_0^* \right| \tag{35}$$

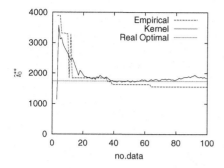

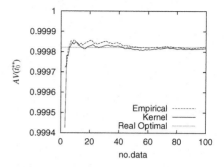

Fig. 3. Asymptotic behavior of estimate of the optimal preventive rejuvenation schedule

Fig. 4. Asymptotic behavior of estimate of the maximum system availability

and

$$\mathrm{RAEA}_{AV} = \frac{1}{mAV(t_0^*)} \sum_{j=1}^{m} \left| AV(\hat{t}_{0_j}^{**}) - AV(t_0^*) \right| . \tag{36}$$

In this experiment, $m = 1,000$ simulation runs are executed with $\gamma = 1.5, 2.0, 4.0$, where $\hat{t}_{0_j}^{**}$ is the optimal periodic preventive rejuvenation schedule estimated in the j-th simulation run. From Figs. 5–10, when the number of sample data is extremely small, the relative absolute error average of estimates of the maximum system availability based on the kernel density estimation is not necessarily outstanding. However, it can be observed that the convergence speed of the optimal preventive rejuvenation schedule by the kernel density method is rather faster than the existing one based on the empirical distribution. The most significant point is that the kernel density estimation is superior to the existing method from the viewpoint of the estimation accuracy. From Fig.7, it is seen that RAEA_{t_0}s based on the

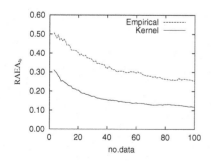

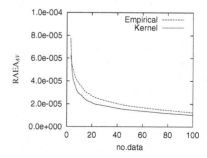

Fig. 5. Relative absolute error average of estimates of the optimal preventive rejuvenation schedule ($\gamma = 1.5$)

Fig. 6. Relative absolute error average of estimates of the maximum system availability ($\gamma = 1.5$)

empirical distribution and the kernel density methods, are 25.7% and 23.5%, respectively, when 20 failure time data are observed. Also, from Fig. 8, RAEA_{AV}s based on the empirical and the kernel methods are 0.0023% and 0.0019%. Hence the RAEA_{t_0} and RAEA_{AV} can be improved 8.6% and 17.4% in respective cases. Therefore, it can be concluded that the statistical estimation algorithm based on the kernel density estimation can improve the convergence speed of the estimate. This enables us to apply the proposed estimation algorithm to the actual fault management for an operational software system with high availability requirement.

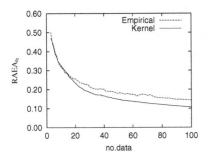

Fig. 7. Relative absolute error average of estimates of the optimal preventive rejuvenation schedule ($\gamma = 2.0$)

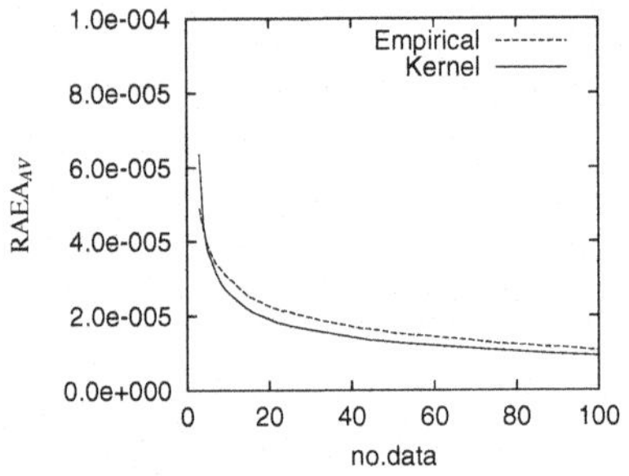

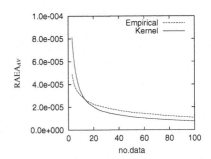

Fig. 8. Relative absolute error average of estimates of the maximum system availability ($\gamma = 2.0$)

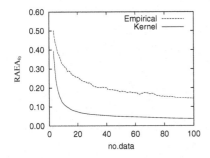

Fig. 9. Relative absolute error average of estimates of the optimal preventive rejuvenation schedule ($\gamma = 4.0$)

Fig. 10. Relative absolute error average of estimates of the maximum system availability ($\gamma = 4.0$)

6   Conclusions

In this paper, we have developed a faster estimation algorithm based on the kernel density estimation for the optimal periodic rejuvenation schedule which maximizes the steady-state system availability. Throughout the Monte Carlo simulation experiments, we have compared the proposed algorithm with the existing one based on the empirical distribution of the system failure time data. It has been shown quantitatively that our approach could improve the existing availability estimation algorithm in terms of convergence speed and was rather effective in the sense that the large sample data are not needed.

In the future, we will further improve the proposed kernel density approach in terms of convergence speed. For instance, although we assumed the Gaussian kernel function and the bandwidth based on MISE, these design factors are not always suitable in every estimation phase. Especially, the selection problem of kernel function is quite sensitive to improve the estimation accuracy and the convergence speed. In fact, several authors tried to improve the kernel density estimator from the various points of view in more generalized statistical inference framework [11], [19]. The optimal design problem to trigger the software rejuvenation should be studied more and more so as to meet the practical requirement on adaptive and autonomic computing.

References

1. Adams, E., 1984. Optimizing preventive service of the software products. *IBM Journal of Research & Development*, **28** (1): 2–14.
2. Avritzer, A. and Weyuker, E. J. 1997. Monitoring smoothly degrading systems for increased dependability. *Empirical Software Engineering*, **2** (1): 59–77.
3. Avritzer, A., Bondi, A., Grottke, M., Weyuker, E. J. and Trivedi, K. S. 2006. Performance assurance via software rejuvenation: monitoring, statistics and algorithms. *Proceedings of International Conference on Dependable Systems and Networks (DSN-2006)*: 435–444, IEEE CS Press.
4. Bao, Y., Sun, X. and Trivedi, K. S. 2003. Adaptive software rejuvenation: degradation model and rejuvenation scheme. *Proceedings of International Conference on Dependable Systems and Networks (DSN-2003)*: 241–248, IEEE CS Press.
5. Bao, Y., Sun, X. and Trivedi, K. S. 2005. A workload-based analysis of software aging, and rejuvenation. *IEEE Transactions on Reliability*, **54** (3): 541–548.
6. Bobbio, A., Sereno, M. and Anglano, C. 2001. Fine grained software degradation models for optimal rejuvenation policies. *Performance Evaluation*, **46** (1): 45–62.
7. Castelli, V., Harper, R. E., Heidelberger, P., Hunter, S. W., Trivedi, K. S., Vaidyanathan, K. V. and Zeggert, W. P. 2001. Proactive management of software aging. *IBM Journal of Research & Development*, **45** (2): 311–332.
8. Cacoullos, T. 1966. Estimation of a multivariate density. *Annals of the Institute of Statistical Mathematics*, **18** (2): 178–189.
9. Dohi, T., Goševa-Popstojanova, K. and Trivedi, K. S. 2001. Estimating software rejuvenation schedule in high assurance systems. *Computer Journal*, **44** (6): 473–485.
10. Dohi, T., Iwamoto, K., Okamura, H. and Kaio, N. 2003. Discrete availability models to rejuvenate a telecommunication billing application. *IEICE Transactions on Communications (B)*, **E86-B** (10), 2931–2939.
11. Duin, R. P. W. (1976). On the choice of smoothing parameters for Parzen estimators of probability density functions. *IEEE Transactions on Computers*, **C-25** (11), 1175–1179.

12. Eto, H. and Dohi, T. 2006. Analysis of a service degradation model with preventive rejuvenation. *Service Availability: Third International Service Availability Symposium (ISAS 2006)* (eds., D. Penkler, M. Reitenspiess and F. Tam), LNCS **4328**, 17–29, Springer-Verlag.

13. Garg, S., Telek, M., Puliafito, A. and Trivedi, K. S. 1995. Analysis of software rejuvenation using Markov regenerative stochastic Petri net. *Proceedings of 6th International Symposium on Software Reliability Engineering (ISSRE-1995)*: 24–27, IEEE CS Press.

14. Garg, S., Pfening, S., Puliafito, A., Telek, M. and Trivedi, K. S. 1998. Analysis of preventive maintenance in transactions based software systems. *IEEE Transactions on Computers*, **47** (1): 96–107.

15. Grottke, M., Lie, L., Vaidyanathan, K. V. and Trivedi, K. S. 2006. Analysis of software aging in a web server. *IEEE Transactions on Reliability*, **55** (3): 411–420.

16. Hoffmann, G. A., Trivedi, K. S. and Malek, M. 2006. A best practice guide to resource forecasting for the Apache webserver. *Proceedings of 12th Pacific Rim International Symposium on Dependable Computing (PRDC-2006)*: 183–193, IEEE CS Press.

17. Huang, Y., Kintala, C., Kolettis, N. and Fulton, N. D. 1995. Software rejuvenation: analysis, module and applications. *Proceedings of 25th International Symposium on Fault Tolerant Computing (FTC-1995)*: 381–390, IEEE CS Press.

18. Iwamoto, K., Dohi, T. and Kaio, N. 2007. Maximizing system availability for operational software systems with periodic rejuvenation. *Journal of Autonomic and Trusted Computing*, (in press).

19. Izenman, A.J. (1991). Recent developments in nonparametric density estimation. *Journal of American Statistical Association*, **86** (413), 205–224.

20. Parzen, E. 1962. On the estimation of a probability density function and the mode. *Annals of Mathematical Statistics*, **33** (3): 1065–1076.

21. Pfening, S., Garg, S., Puliafito, A., Telek, M. and Trivedi, K. S. 1996. Optimal rejuvenation for tolerating soft failure. *Performance Evaluation*, **27/28** (4): 491–506.

22. Reinecke, P., Van Moorsel, A. P. A. and Wolter, K. 2004. A measurement study of the interplay between application level restart and transport protocol. *Service Availability: First International Service Availability Symposium (ISAS 2004)* (eds., M. Malek, M. Manfred and J. Kaiser), LNCS **3335**, 86–100, Springer-Verlag.

23. Rosenblatt, M. 1956. Remarks on some nonparametric estimates of a density function. *Annals of Mathematical Statistics*, **27** (3): 832–837.

24. Rinsaka, K. and Dohi, T. 2005. Behavioral analysis of fault-tolerant software systems with rejuvenation. *IEICE Transactions on Information and Systems (D)*, **E88-D** (12): 2681–2690.

25. Shereshevsky, M., Crowell, J., Cukic, B. Gandikota, V. and Liu, Y. 2003. Software aging and multifractality of memory resources. *Proceedings of International Conference on Dependable Systems and Networks (DSN-2003)*: 721–730, IEEE CS Press.

26. Silverman, B. W. 1986. *Density Estimation for Statistics and Data Analysis*, Chapman and Hall.

27. Suzuki, H., Dohi, T., Goševa-Popstojanova, K. and Trivedi, K. S. 2002. Analysis of multi step failure models with periodic software rejuvenation. *Advances in Stochastic Modelling* (eds., J. R. Artalejo and A. Krishnamoorthy): 85–108, Notable Publications.

28. Tai, A. T., Alkalai, L. and Chau, S. N. 1999. On-board preventive maintenance: a design-oriented analytic study for long-life applications. *Performance Evaluation*, **35** (3/4): 215–232.
29. Vaidyanathan, K. V. and Trivedi, K. S. 2005. A comprehensive model for software rejuvenation. *IEEE Transactions on Dependable and Secure Computing*, **2** (2): 124–137.
30. van Moorsel, A. P. A. and Wolter, K. 2006. Analysis of restart mechanisms in software systems. *IEEE Transactions on Software Engineering*, **32** (8): 547–558.
31. Wang, D., Xie, W. and Trivedi, K. S. 2007. Performability analysis of clustered systems with rejuvenation under varying workload. *Performance Evaluation*, (in press).
32. Yurcik, W. and Doss, D. 2001. Achieving fault-tolerant software with rejuvenation and reconfiguration. *IEEE Software*, **18** (4): 48–52.

An Eclipse-Based Framework for AIS Service Configurations

András Kövi[1,2] and Dániel Varró[1,2]

[1] Department of Measurement and Information Systems
Budapest University of Technology and Economics
H-1117, Magyar Tudsok krt. 2, Budapest, Hungary
kovi@mit.bme.hu
[2] OptXware Research & Development LLC.
H-1137, Katona J. u. 39., Budapest, Hungary
varro@mit.bme.hu

Abstract. In the paper, we propose an Eclipse-based model-driven framework to support an integrated development, analysis and deployment of Application Interface Specification (AIS) service configurations. Service configurations are first captured by platform-independent models (PIM), which directly correspond to the AIS standard itself, and abstract from vendor-specific details. Specificities of vendor-specific AIS middleware are incorporated into platform-specific models (PSM), which are derived from PIMs by automatic model transformations. Model analysis can be carried out either on the PIM-level to ensure standard compliance of a given service configuration, or on the PSM-level to detect availability bottlenecks by formal analysis early in the service configuration design. Finally, deployment descriptors of the selected AIS platform are generated from verified service configurations by automatic code generation techniques.

1 Introduction

As the range of business functionality is rapidly increasing to better meet customer needs, quality requirements are increasingly important in addition to rapid time-to-market development cycles. Availability, i.e. the continuity of a service, is one of the most important factors in the overall quality of business-intensive services.

However, in order to meet availability requirements, a service needs to be designed for availability by using well-founded development techniques. In order to avoid the re-development of best-practice solutions for achieving high availability, architectural-level solutions have been proposed based on best practices of constructing dependable systems.

The specifications of the Service Availability Forum. The *Service Availability* *TM Forum (SAF)* [32] aims at providing standardized solutions for making services highly available. The *Application Interface Specification (AIS)* of the Forum defines the standard interfaces for accessing Highly Available (HA)

M. Malek et al.(Eds.): ISAS 2007, LNCS 4526, pp. 110–126, 2007.
© Springer-Verlag Berlin Heidelberg 2007

middleware and infrastructure services that reside logically between applications and the operating system.

The entities defined in the AIS specifications (e.g. service units, message queues, applications, etc.) are described semi-formally by the *Information Model (IM)* in the form of UML classes [12]. The *Information Model Management Service (IMM)* [14] is the service in AIS that provides a set of APIs and administrative operations to create, access and manage the objects of the IM.

In the SA Forum ecosystem the *Software Management Framework (SwMF)* [15] provides all the functionality to migrate a system configuration to a desired new one. During the migration both the IM is updated and the required software entities are installed.

Problem statement. Although the classes in the IM define the common concepts that are used to build up SAF AIS compliant applications, standard descriptions do not alone guarantee that a certain service configuration will meet its quality of service (QoS) requirements. Moreover, the portability of service configurations between different commercial-off-the-shelf (COTS) AIS middleware implementations is problematic, i.e. deployment of a service configuration to a certain middleware makes it inappropriate for another AIS platform without changes, mainly due to the lack of standardization for the description of service configurations.

Objectives. In this paper we argue for the use of model-driven development techniques in the context of services to overcome the problems above. For this purpose, we present an Eclipse-based framework, which simultaneously supports the model-based development, analysis and deployment of SAF AIS compliant services. More specifically,

1. we propose modeling tools for describing AIS service configurations either by domain-specific modeling or using a UML Profile (see Sec. 3);
2. we present analysis tools to detect non-compliancy of a certain service configuration to the AIS standard, and highlight QoS bottlenecks in a configuration by using formal analysis tools (see Sec. 4);
3. finally, we demonstrate how automatic code generation and model transformation techniques can be used to derive vendor-specific deployment descriptors for service configurations (see Sec. 5).

2   An Overview of the Approach

In the following, we present an architectural overview of our framework to summarize its major components (see Fig. 1). Later, each of these components will be described in detail.

Modeling of AIS service configurations. We propose to adapt a model-driven development approach for AIS service configurations. For this purpose, *platform independent models (PIM)* of services are first constructed in accordance with the requirements specification. A well-formed PIM should conform

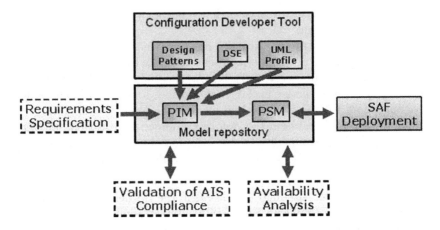

Fig. 1. Architecture overview

to the metamodel of the AIS standard itself. In a subsequent step, *platform-specific models (PSM)* corresponding to AIS middleware of a specific vendor can be derived automatically by model transformations. These models are captured either by a domain-specific editor for AIS models based on the *Eclipse Modeling Framework (EMF)*, or using a UML Profile for AIS services embedded into the off-the-shelf UML tool of IBM Rational Software Architect. Best practices of creating service configurations are grouped into design pattern libraries, which are made available to service architects.

Model analysis. The metamodel of the AIS standard can be complemented with constraints, defined in the Object Constraint Language (OCL), which capture additional well-formedness rules of the AIS standard in a formal way. When a PIM of a service configuration is available in the form of an EMF model, its conformance to the standard can be checked by validating the OCL constraints on the PIM (Sec. 3.2) using the OCL validation framework of EMF. Assuming that, HA parameters of a certain AIS platform are available for the designer, the PSM (Sec. 3.4) of a service configuration can be annotated with these service parameters. Based upon such an annotation, we can carry out formal analysis to detect availability bottlenecks early in the service development process by transforming the PSM of a service configuration into General Stochastic Petri Nets (Sec. 4.1), and analyzing different characteristics of those petri nets.

Service deployment. After analyzing a service configuration for a given AIS middleware, the actual deployment descriptors of the service configuration can be generated by automated code generation techniques, such as Java Emission Templates (JET) (Sec. 5).

The toolkit. This integrated model-driven development framework is based on standard, open interfaces as provided by Eclipse, and especially, the Eclipse Modeling Framework (EMF). The advantage of using Eclipse and EMF for the implementation is that there is a wide spectrum of tools that facilitate development for the Eclipse platform, moreover, EMF has become the de-facto standard for model exchange in the industry nowadays. EMF is capable of generating the editor code and an example editor program for our metamodel that reduces the development time and the possibility of programming faults. In addition, EMF facilitates the validation of models, which will be described later in Sec. 4.

3   Modeling of Service Configurations

3.1   Requirements Specification

The service configuration development workflow starts with gathering requirements for service deployment. This information includes the type and number of components, the definition of services, service groups and the application itself. Since system resources for deployment are finite, priorities between services should be set up based upon the required availability for different services as part of the requirements specification.

There are well established schemes for defining the requirements of applications in specific application domains, however, it is still an open issue how these requirements can automatically be incorporated into the service configuration in the general case. Therefore, this phase of developing service configurations for AIS middleware is subject to future work.

3.2   Platform Independent Model (PIM)

In a model-driven approach, the development of service deployment configuration commences with the creation of a Platform Independent Model (PIM), which is the AIS configuration of the service. This PIM model of a service configuration is independent of the underlying platform implementation, thus it can be reused for different AIS platforms.

This PIM serves multiple purposes:

- it is used to integrate the service into the SAF ecosystem
- it is the input for the deployment procedure
- it can serve as input for generation of the source code of the service to speed up application implementation

Attributes and relations of conceptual AIS elements (service groups, service units, etc.) and other resources that are used by the service, for example, message queues and log streams, should be set up in this step.

AIS-PIM metamodel. The metamodel of the PIM (PIMM) of an AIS compliant application is built up from the entities defined in the specifications, thus, it ensures the compliance of the configuration model to the standard itself. As discussed in Sec. 1, the SA Forum Information Model (IM) contains a UML representation of service entities, e.g. it contains the Service Unit class that is

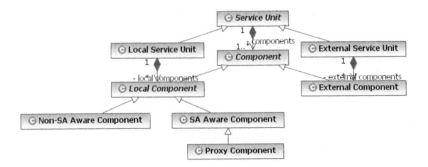

Fig. 2. Service unit and component class hierarchy

used to represent a service unit. Therefore, we have chosen the IM to serve as the basis of our PIM metamodel.

However, the Information Model, as defined by the SA Forum, is unable to identify certain semantic relations between service entities. For instance, issues like which service is the owner of a message queue or which log stream is opened by which application, are not represented in the IM model. Furthermore, for clarity purposes, we used the ontology listed in the AMF specification (Sec. 3.2 Logical Entities of [13]), which explicitly represents the type hierarchy of components and services, rather than the simple aggregated class concept used in the UML model of the IM. We believe that, the clarity of the AIS metamodel is highly improved by these changes.

The modified component and service unit hierarchy is depicted in Fig. 2. The general *Component* class is specialized into *Local Component* and *External Component* classes by classifying components according to the location of the

Fig. 3. Example model with stereotypes

component from the point of view of the *AMF cluster*. Then the *Local Component* is further specialized into *Non-SA Aware Component* and *SA Aware Component* classes. Finally, the specialized case of the *SA Aware Component* is the *Proxy Component*, which corresponds to the proxy components in AMF. On the other hand, the *Service Unit* class is specialized into two descendant classes: the *Local Service Unit* and the *External Service Unit* class. A *Local Service Unit* contains only *Local Components* while the *External Service Unit* comprises only *External Components*.

Because of the generality of the *Component*, *Service Unit* and *Local Component* classes, their usage in service configuration models is not allowed; and thus to avoid their instantiation, they are made abstract.

In Fig 3 a valid service configuration example is depicted. The class of the objects is indicated by the stereotypes, e.g. *Local Service Unit*, *Proxy Component*, etc.

Since this paper intends to give an overview of our framework and the techniques we use in it, only the most important changes to the metamodel are listed in the following:

- *Component class extended with reference attributes to all types of SAF resources* (e.g. message queue, lock, log stream) to support the indication of resource usage.
- *Runtime attributes*, that store the runtime state of the object, *are deleted from the classes* since such information is useless at design time. E.g. the attribute that stores the administrative state of a component or the one that contains the number of restarts of a service unit is removed.

3.3   Design Patterns

Building up the PIM manually from scratch can be a time consuming and error prone task. In an ideal case, a previously elaborated solution for a specific problem can be reused with changing some parameters. To help the developer in such cases design patterns are offered by our framework.

There are two types of design patterns for PIM development:

- **Fault tolerance related patterns** speed up modeling by providing parameterized procedures for automatic creation of ordinary objects and setting up their attributes,
- **AMF best practice patterns** are previously elaborated and stored solutions for more complex problems in certain application domains.

Fault tolerance (FT) related patterns help *create and configure all the necessary objects for a given fault tolerant architecture*. For example, if one creates a service group with 2N redundancy model then there will surely be at least two service units in that service group. Similarly, such "preconfigured" solutions can be provided to the user for all redundancy models defined in the AMF specification.

Another useful group of FT related design patterns are in connection with the topic of *software redundancy*. We talk about software redundancy when the simple multiplication of components in a service deployment does not provide sufficient fault tolerance, especially, against faults in the software. Such protection is essential for mission critical systems where erroneous behavior of a component can lead to catastrophic results. There are generally used patterns for these problems, e.g. *N-version programming (NVP)* [1] or *N self configuring programming (NSCP)* [23]. These redundancy schemes can be applied on SAF AMF managed software systems as well. As an example in the followings we show how the NVP scheme can be used.

In the NVP scheme several software variants compute simultaneously the same job/request, and when all of them are ready, a voter makes the decision on the final result.

Let us assume that we have three different software variants and want to use them in an NVP scheme (see Fig. 4). An SAF compliant service needs the following entities for this scheme: separate *Service Unit* for the *execution environment*,

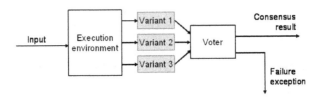

Fig. 4. NVP scheme for three software variants

for *each variant* and the *voter*, separate *Service Groups* for the *different functionality groups*, and finally, *message queues* are necessary for communication.

In Fig. 5 the AMF configuration for the described scheme is depicted. The *execution environment* sends the input requests through the *message queues* prefixed "*In_*" to the *respective variants* and the *variants* send their results to the *voter* through the "*Out_* queues. (Note that, not all usage relations and AMF components are visible in the figure to prevent making it unnecessarily complicated.)

AMF configuration for all the previously mentioned software redundancy schemes can be defined in an akin way.

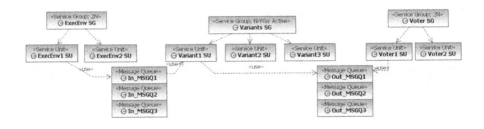

Fig. 5. AMF configuration for NVP scheme with three variants

AMF best practices. The other group of design patterns is best practices, which contain *previously stored system architectures and implementation related solutions for certain application domains*. System architectures can be for example, configurations for sensor networks or different systems that need a given level of reliability or availability. These best practices can have parameters as well that make them more flexible and more widely reusable (e.g. the number of sensors, data collectors, monitoring systems, etc).

3.4   Platform Specific Model (PSM)

Although the specifications of AIS standardize the interfaces an application may use to access the HA services of the middleware, there may be differences between platform/middleware implementations in the sense that how they are configured, and which services and functionalities are implemented. Thus, it is advantageous to create a *Platform Specific Metamodel (PSMM)* for each platform implementation.

Platform Specific Metamodel (PSMM). This metamodel *contains all the entities and their relations in the given platform implementation.* These entities may have extended or restricted features compared to the corresponding entities of the PIM metamodel. Furthermore, there may be additional entities for non standard services that a vendor-specific AIS implementation provides.

Using the notions of the PSMM the *Platform Specific Model (PSM)* of the service (*Service PSM*) can be created that describes a service configuration on the given platform implementation. However, the PSM of the service is preferably not created from scratch every time it is deployed to a different platform. If the PIM of the service exists it can be transformed into a PSM using a specific PIM to PSM mapping. The model transformation describes which element or elements in the PIM are mapped into which element(s) in the PSM model. (Technical details of such model transformations are discussed in Sec. 3.5)

3.5   Implementation Details

In the previous sections we described the configuration development workflow and its elements. A tool that facilitates this workflow has to provide a user interface that exposes all the required functionalities for creating, modifying, verifying, validating and transforming the introduced models. This user interface is called the modeling front-end.

The modeling front-end. UML is one possible language that we use to create service configuration models. UML provides a wide range of extension mechanisms (stereotypes, tagged values, etc.) to customize the basic language, and create domain specific dialects. A *UML profile* is the notion that encapsulates all the extensions of a specific dialect. We created a UML profile for AIS, i.e. a dialect, that contains stereotypes corresponding to the entity types of the AIS specifications, e.g. local service unit, service group, local component. An example for a stereotyped model created with IBM Rational Software Architect can be seen in Fig. 6.

Service models. Representation of the Eclipse Modeling Framework (EMF) [8] is the de facto industrial standard for storing and manipulating models in Eclipse. Metamodels in EMF are called Ecore models. The EMF model development workflow starts with *the creation of the metamodel* (i.e. an Ecore model). In our case it is the metamodel of the PIM and the PSMs. Then we *use the automatic code generation facility* that generates us the Java classes for the model, the model editor API, a sample model editor and class stubs for testing. EMF Ecore models are stored in XML files and this assures their easy reusability in other, non EMF based applications as well. EMF provides automated support for loading and serializing models from metamodel-specific XML formats corresponding to the XMI 2.0 standard. These EMF models can also serve as the basis of model validation as described in Sec. 3.

Domain Specific Model Editor. Domain specific model editors are generated editors, which are customized for specific application domains. In the Eclipse environment there are specific frameworks that provide means to easily develop domain specific model editors. Most widely used and best elaborated is the *Graphical Editing Framework (GEF)* [9], which provides APIs for the creation of graphical editors. Since most editors provide the same functionalities, only the context and the outlook differs in many cases, the *Graphical Modeling Framework (GMF)* [10] has been started to support the development of rich domain-specific model editors. GMF provides means to define different aspects of the editor using specific models, and then automatically generate the source code for it.

Design patterns. Using the automatically generated specific model editor API, the modification of PIM and PSM models is possible from code. The design patterns library uses this AIS specific API to carry out a sequence of model manipulation operations. In our initial framework, design patterns are implemented as simple parameterized methods (without graphical user interface). Application of a design pattern on a model is done by calling the respective method with specific parameters.

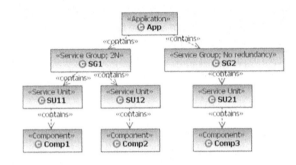

Fig. 6. Example stereotyped service configuration model

Model transformations. As mentioned above, model transformation is the mean that is used to generate the PSM from the PIM or the platform specific deployment descriptors from the PSM. The VIATRA2 transformation framework provides such model transformations by combining the formal paradigms of abstract state machines and graph transformation, which provide a rule and pattern based manipulation of models. As model transformations are out of the scope of this paper, here we do not describe them in detail. For more information on this topic see [34, 2].

4   Model Analysis

4.1   Static Analysis of Service Configuration Models

After creating a service configuration model, it is essential to verify its compliance with the AIS standard. This is carried out by formal verification of the model against constraints that are defined in its metamodel. These *well-formedness and semantic constraints* come from various requirements, e.g. *multiplicity restrictions* or *attribute values*, or a constraint may be composed of (i.e. it may refer to) *other constraints* as well. In Fig. 7 the types of model element constraints and the direction of possible implications are depicted, while Fig. 8 shows an example for each type of constraint implication.

Object Constraint Language.
For specifying constraints in object oriented models the Object Constraint Language (OCL) [26] of OMG [19] is a widely used standard formalism. It can be used to express additional constraints on metamodels that cannot be expressed, or are very difficult to express, with the metamodel itself.

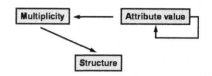

Fig. 7. Types of model element constraints. The arrows indicate the possible directions of implication.

Metamodel constraints. The OCL constraints are defined on the classes of the metamodel and their attributes. To ensure the correctness of the model we have to define constraints in the following cases:

1. *Value range restrictions for attributes.* (E.g. the size of the message queue (saMsgQueueSize attrib.) has to be greater than zero)
2. *Structural multiplicity restrictions.* (E.g. number of SUs in an SG)
3. *Attribute dependencies* where the value of one attribute depends on the value of some other attributes. E.g. if the component capability model of a component (saAmfCompCapability attribute) is *x_active_and_y_standby* then the maximum number of standby component service instances should be greater than zero (saAmfCompMaxStandbyCsi attribute).

Source	Destination	Example
Attr	Attr	The redundancy model of the service group (SG) (defined by the *asAmfSGRedundancyModel* attribute of the corresponding class) prescribes the required capabilities of a component. (E.g in a SG with N-Way redundancy model all components have to implement the *x_active_and_y_standby* component capability model.)
Attr	Multip	Redundancy model of the service group (SG) can define the lower multiplicity (i.e. the minimum number) of service units (SUs). (E.g. the 2N redundancy model supposes the existence of at least two service units.)
Multip	Struct	Each service unit of a service group should be deployed to different nodes in order to provide protection against node failures.

Fig. 8. Examples for different constraints

4. *Association dependencies.* E.g. service unit - service instance relations through the rankedSUs attribute.

In the following, we show two example OCLs on the PIMM. First, the simple example for *value range restriction constraint* is the *relative distinguished name* (RDN) constraint for *name attribute of the component* class, which describes that there cannot be two *components* with identical names in a *service unit*:

```
context ServiceUnit inv :
self.components -> forAll(c1, c2 |
        c1 <> c2 implies c1.name <> c2.name)
```

The respective part of the metamodel is depicted in Fig. 9. RDN constraints have to be stated for many other elements as well, like service groups, service units, etc.

A more complex sample OCL is the "*service types checking*" constraint for service instances:

```
context ServiceInstance inv :
if self.rankedSUs -> notEmpty then
  let requiredCSTs : Set<CSType> =
    self.csis.csType -> asSet() in
      self.rankedSUs -> forAll( su : ServiceUnit |
        su.components.csTypes ->
          asSet() -> includesAll(requiredCSTs)
      )
endif
```

The "*service types checking*" verifies that whether each *service unit* that the *service instance* is assigned to, by the ranked service units (*rankedSUs*) attribute, provides every *service type* the *service instance* requires. This constraint is a required condition for the successful assignment of the given *service instance*. The referenced part of the metamodel is depicted in Fig. 10.

Implementation. Checking of OCL constraints in an EMF based tool can be carried out by using the EMF OCL and Validation frameworks. At the time of writing the article there was no stable release of the mentioned frameworks, therefore,

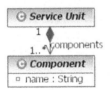

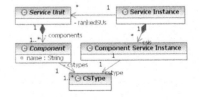

Fig. 9. Relation of service unit and component class

Fig. 10. Relation of service unit and service instance

most of the checks were actually (re)implemented in plain Java. However, the next EMF release, the Eclipse Modeling Framework Technologies (EMFT), promises to support the validation of OCL constraints over EMF models.

4.2 Non-functional Analysis

For users it is always a problem that the correctness of the configuration does not assure the appropriate functionality of the system.

Unfortunately, the compliance of a service configuration to the AIS standard does not alone guarantee that the quality of service requirements are met by the service configuration after deployment. For example, in high availability systems the expected availability and reliability of a service is a major parameter that has to satisfy certain required levels. Another problem is that during the installation of the new services some parts of the system may temporarily go down, however, the continuity of services has to be maintained in these periods as well, and this fact imposes constraints on the upgrade scenarios.

For these reasons, our framework supports *formal analysis of availability* as well. Often analysis techniques and tools can be integrated likewise.

Availability and reliability analysis. In HA systems the most important measures are the *availability* and *reliability* of the services. Standard dependability analysis techniques can be used to determine the value of these measures in a particular system to detect quality bottlenecks early in the design. In [24] the design, implementation and application of a tool is described that is able to *construct automatically a dependability model* (in the form of Generalized Stochastic Petri Nets) from a system architecture model. Then the *dependability model can be solved by an external solver* (e.g. the SPNP package [6]), computing in this way the system-level reliability or availability measures. The input for the tool is the stereotyped UML model of the system. In our case the PSM is adopted to the input of the tool chain by simple, rather syntactic model transformations, e.g. annotation by stereotypes, indication of usage dependencies, etc.

5 Automated Generation of Configurations

In the last phase of the configuration development we have to obtain the PSM of the deployed service configuration (*Deployment PSM* later), and then merge it with the *Service PSM*. The final step is the generation of the platform specific deployment descriptors using the *Merged PSM*.

In the following, first we discuss the solutions for reengineering a deployment configuration into a PSM, then we introduce different technologies and methods that are used for configuration generation.

5.1 Reengineering a Deployed Configuration

Before a new service could be integrated into an existing deployment the Deployment PSM has to be created. The following methods are available for reengineering the currently deployed service configuration:

1. Using model transformations the deployment descriptors are derived into a Deployment PSM
2. An IMM revealer agent traverses through the configuration tree and returns the Deployment PSM as the result of a request.

PSM creation by transformations. To eliminate the human faults, such as mistyping or misunderstanding the model, *model transformations are used for automatic generation of the Service PSM.* Moreover, the system deployment configuration files are not standardized, thus, *vendor specific transformations have to be written for each platform implementation.* Such transformations can be implemented, for instance, in the VIATRA2 model transformation framework [34] in the form of importer plugins and graph transformations. As model transformations is a complex topic and does not connect inherently to the subject of this paper, here we do not deal with it, but more information can be found in [24].

IMM revealer agent. In systems where the IMM service is available *a component can be written that traverses the Information Model and returns the Deployment PSM.* As mentioned in Sec. 3.5 Ecore models, and thus the PSMs as well, are stored in an XML format. As a consequence, *the agent simply has to return the PSM XML, which can instantly be used by the configuration developer tool* without any modifications.

5.2   Generating the Deployment Descriptors

The final step of the model-driven configuration development process is the *generation of platform specific deployment descriptors.* In Eclipse we can use *Java Emitter Templates (JET)* [11] for code generation from EMF models. JET is an easy to use and effective tool to generate the structured, platform specific configuration descriptor files automatically from the PSMs. JET templates take an object as input and produce formatted text using the different properties and attributes of the input object. These templates use a simple JSP [33] like syntax to describe the format of the output text.

In our case, the *Merged PSM is passed to the templates as parameter*, and the *resulting text is saved into a file.* Separate JET templates need to be created for each different output configuration file. An example JET template is listed in the following.

Listing 1.1. Example JET template

```
<%@ jet package=" hello "  class=" GreetingTemplate "
                        skeleton=" generator . skeleton " %>
<%AISModel  model  =  (AISModel) argument ;
    foreach (SAFApp  app  in  model . Applications )  {%>
        <%=app . safApp%>,
    <%}%>
```

Alternatively, we could also use the code generation features of VIATRA2 for the same task.

6   Related Work

Model-driven development for Web services. The work presented in this paper was influenced by several proposals in different fields. First, proposals for the *model-driven development of service configurations have already been elaborated for Web services*, which have certain similarities with the SA Forum service configurations that we deal with, e.g. a complete framework based on the high-level modeling of Web services and their interactions with Web applications is described in [25]. In [18] a method is described for importing Web service descriptions into UML models, then integrating them, and finally generating the XML descriptors for the composite Web service. This process is similar to our approach to the integration of PSMs into a Merged PSM.

As we stated in Sec. 3.1 there are solutions for *integrating some specific requirements into service configurations*. As an example, a methodology is described for incorporating reliability attributes into Web service configurations in [17]. Furthermore, this process is carried out with model transformations using the VIATRA2 transformation framework. Other approaches that use model transformations for the integration of non-functional requirements can be found in [7,31] and [22].

However, these solutions are different from our approach in that (i) only parts of the development process are supported and (ii) since Web service configurations have a standardized format the generation of platform specific descriptors is not an issue.

Non-functional model-driven analysis for services. We have used basic principles that are described in [5] and [24] for defining the model constraints, and carrying out the validation of the Service PSM models. Another solution for reliability prediction of a system based on UML models is described in [30]. They extend the Schedulability Performance and Time (SPT) UML profile [20] then perform analysis with transforming the UML model into a labeled transition system (LTS) using XML-based transformations. This solution sticks more to the standards based model-driven approach by using the standardized UML-XML mappings. However, the adaptability of the SPT Profile for AIS based services is unclear. Additional techniques for model-transformation based analysis of non-functional properties of service configurations are presented in [16,3]. Finally, a method is introduced in [4] for generating optimal deployment configurations to a definite set of server nodes that guarantees the required availability and performance characteristics for all services.

Eclipse based configuration development tools. During our research we found only the OpenClovis IDE as an available Eclispe-based configuration developer tool for an AIS compliant platform,. The OpenClovis IDE [28] implements a subset of the functionalities that we proposed in this paper, e.g. creating and modifying AIS configuration models, generating source code and template based configuration development. The main difference between our proposal and the

OpenClovis IDE is that the latter implements only platform specific parts of the toolchain for the OpenClovis Application Service Platform middleware [27].

Our contribution. As a summary, the novelty of our approach compared to the previously enumerated works is that we define (i) *a complete model-driven methodology for service configuration development* (ii) *dedicated to the SA Forum ecosystem*, (iii) by developing a *toolchain using Eclipse-based technologies*. As a result, we defined a flexible toolkit that can easily be adopted to different needs of different platform implementations, meanwhile helping the developers with standard compliant platform independent model development for highly available service configurations. Even if some components of our framework are in an early prototype phase, we believe that the current paper provides relevant specification for future improvements.

7   Conclusions

In this paper, we presented an integrated model-driven configuration development method for AIS services and described a prototype toolchain that supports this process. Furthermore, we showed how such a tool can be implemented on the basis of Eclipse frameworks.

Although the specifications of AIS define the entities of the system and operations that an application may invoke, the format of the service configuration has not been standardized. Thus, the configuration of different platform implementations can be widely different. So as to support the modeling of the platform independent and platform specific views of the service configuration, we defined the Platform Independent Model and the Platform Specific Model. We use automatic model transformations for the PIM to PSM transformation as well, as transformations for model validation to speed up these processes, and to avoid human errors. Finally, the deployment descriptors for a given platform can automatically be generated from the PSM.

In the future we consider the following improvements:

- **Semantics-based model analysis.** Currently we define OCL constraints on the metamodel and then check them using the code generated by the EMFT-OCL framework. The problem with this approach is that, if a new constraint is introduced or an existing one is modified the validation code has to be regenerated or rewritten. Ontology-based model analysis provides a code-independent way for validating constraints. In ontology-based model analysis we define a formal ontology, which contains the metamodel as a T-Box (Terminology Box) and the model as an A-Box (Assertion Box). Then the ontology is passed to a reasoner like RACER [29] that decides whether the ontology is consistent or not. Simple OCL constraints can be implemented in the T-Box, while complex constraints are verified by using model queries. Such model analysis architecture provides more flexibility, however, it is restricted to a select of OCLs.

   – **Integration of SwMF.** We think it is important to be able to generate standardized configuration descriptors as well (besides platform specific descriptors) that can be used by systems implementing the Software Management Framework (SwMF). Thus, we consider the development of a transformation for PIM that provides the essential *Entity types file*, which is used to describe the software entities that are delivered by a software bundle.

Acknowledgements

This work was partially supported by the HIDENETS project [21] of the European Union.

References

1. A. Avizienis. The methodology of n-version programming, 1995.
2. A. Balogh, A. Németh, A. Schmidt, I. Ráth, D. Vágó, D. Varró, and A. Pataricza. The VIATRA2 model transformation framework. In *ECMDA 2005 – Tools Track*, 2005.
3. A. Balogh and A. Pataricza. Quality-of-service analysis of dependable application models. 2006. Accepted for the 5th International Workshop on Critical Systems Development Using Modeling Languages (CSDUML 2006).
4. András Balogh, Dániel Varró, and András Pataricza. Model-based optimization of enterprise application and service deployment. In *ISAS*, pages 84–98, 2005.
5. Luciano Baresi, Reiko Heckel, Sebastian Thöne, and Dániel Varró. Style-based modeling and refinement of service-oriented architectures. *Software and Systems Modeling*, 5(2):187–207, June 2006.
6. Gianfranco Ciardo, Kishor S. Trivedi, and et al. Spnp: Stochastic petri net package - version 5.0.
7. Vittorio Cortellessa, Antinisca Di Marco, and Paola Inverardi. Software performance model-driven architecture. In *SAC '06: Proceedings of the 2006 ACM symposium on Applied computing*, pages 1218–1223, New York, NY, USA, 2006. ACM Press.
8. Eclipse modeling framework. `http://www.eclipse.org/modeling/`.
9. Graphical editing framework. `http://www.eclipse.org/gef/`.
10. Graphical modeling framework. `http://www.eclipse.org/gmf/`.
11. Java emitter templates. `http://www.eclipse.org/emft/projects/jet/`.
12. Service Availability™Forum. *Information Model Classes, SAI-XMI-A.01.01*, 2005.
13. Service Availability™Forum. *Availability Management Framework, SAI-AIS-B.01.02*, February 2006.
14. Service Availability™Forum. *Information Model Management Service, SAI-AIS-B.01.02*, February 2006.
15. Service Availability™Forum. *Software Management Framework, SAI-AIS-A.01.01.02 draft version*, 2007.
16. László Gönczy. Dependability analysis and synthesis of web services. In *Proc. 13th PhD Mini-Symposium*, Budapest, Hungary, 2004.
17. László Gönczy, János Ávéd, and Dániel Varró. Model-based deployment of web services to standards-compliant middleware. In Immaculada J. Martinez Pedro Isaias, Miguel Baptista Nunes, editor, *Proc. of the Iadis International Conference on WWW/Internet 2006(ICWI2006)*. Iadis Press, 2006.

18. Roy Gronmo, David Skogan, Ida Solheim, and Jon Oldevik. Model-driven web services development. *eee*, 00:42–45, 2004.
19. Object Management Group. *Object Constraint Language specification.*
    http://omg.org/technology/documents/formal/ocl.htm.
20. Object Management Group. *UML Profile for Schedulability, Performance and Time Specification*, January 2005.
    http://www.omg.org/technology/documents/formal/schedulability.htm.
21. Highly DEpendable ip-based NETworks and Services. http://hidenets.aau.dk.
22. Henk Jonkers, Maria-Eugenia Iacob, Marc M. Lankhorst, and Patrick Strating. Integration and analysis of functional and non-functional aspects in model-driven e-service development. In *EDOC*, pages 229–238, 2005.
23. Jean-Claude Laprie, Christian Béounes, and Karama Kanoun. Definition and analysis of hardware- and software-fault-tolerant architectures. *Computer*, 23(7):39–51, 1990.
24. I. Majzik, P. Domokos, and M. Magyar. Tool-supported dependability evaluation of redundant architectures in computer based control systems. In E. Schnieder and G. Tarnai, editors, *FORMS/FORMAT 2007, the 6th Symposium on Formal Methods for Automation and Safety in Railway and Automotive Systems, 25-26 January 2007*, pages 342–352, GZVB, Braunschweig, Germany, 2007. ISBN 13:978-3-937655-09-3.
25. Ioana Manolescu, Marco Brambilla, Stefano Ceri, Sara Comai, and Piero Fraternali. Model-driven design and deployment of service-enabled web applications. *ACM Trans. Inter. Tech.*, 5(3):439–479, 2005.
26. Object Management Group. http://omg.org.
27. OpenClovis. Application service platform (asp), release 2.2.
    http://www.openclovis.org/project/asp.
28. OpenClovis. Openclovis ide. http://www.openclovis.org/project/ide.
29. Renamed abox and concept expression reasoner (RACER).
    http://www.racer-systems.com/.
30. Genaina Rodrigues, David Rosenblum, and Sebastian Uchitel. Reliability prediction in model driven development. In *ACM/IEEE 8th International Conference on Model Driven Engineering Languages and Systems*, 2005.
31. Simone Rttger and Steffen Zschaler. Model-driven development for non-functional properties: Refinement through model transformation.
32. Service Availability[TM]Forum. http://saforum.org.
33. Java server pages. http://java.sun.com/products/jsp/.
34. VIATRA2 Framework, an Eclipse GMT subproject.
    http://www.eclipse.org/gmt/.

MDDPro: Model-Driven Dependability Provisioning in Enterprise Distributed Real-Time and Embedded Systems*

Sumant Tambe[1], Jaiganesh Balasubramanian[1], Aniruddha Gokhale[1], and Thomas Damiano[2]

[1] Vanderbilt University, Nashville, TN, USA
{sutambe,jai,gokhale}@dre.vanderbilt.edu
[2] MITRE Corporation

Abstract. Service oriented architecture (SOA) design principles are increasingly being adopted to develop distributed real-time and embedded (DRE) systems, such as avionics mission computing, due to the availability of real-time component middleware platforms. Traditional approaches to fault tolerance that rely on replication and recovery of a single server or a single host do not work in this paradigm since the fault management schemes must now account for the timely and simultaneous failover of groups of entities while improving system availability by minimizing the risk of simultaneous failures of replicated entities. This paper describes MDDPro, a model-driven dependability provisioning tool for DRE systems. MDDPro provides intuitive modeling abstractions to specify failover requirements of DRE systems at different granularities. MDDPro enables plugging in different replica placement algorithms to improve system availability. Finally, its generative capabilities automate the deployment and configuration of the DRE system on the underlying platforms.

Keywords: Dependability Design Tools, Model-Driven Engineering, Generative programming, Real-time SOA systems.

1 Introduction

Dependability is a crucial design consideration for mission-critical distributed real-time and embedded (DRE) systems, such as avionics mission computing, and supervisory control and data acquisition (SCADA) systems. DRE systems development processes are increasingly adopting the service oriented architecture (SOA) design principles due in large part to the availability of real-time component middleware platforms, such as the Lightweight CORBA Component Model (LwCCM) [1]. The SOA approach when applied to DRE systems gives rise to what we term *enterprise DRE systems*, which are a loose coupling of interacting

---

* This work is supported in part or whole by subcontracts from LMCO ATL and BBN for the DARPA Adaptive and Reflective Middleware Systems Program.

M. Malek et al.(Eds.): ISAS 2007, LNCS 4526, pp. 127–144, 2007.
© Springer-Verlag Berlin Heidelberg 2007

real-time and embedded services that are composed, assembled, deployed and configured on the underlying platforms to realize the end-to-end functionality. With the newer SOA-style design, however, new challenges emerge in the design of dependability management solutions for enterprise DRE systems, which stem from the following limitations of contemporary mechanisms:

Limitations of existing dependability mechanisms. A substantial amount of research in dependable distributed computing has predominantly concentrated on providing fault tolerance solutions to intrinsically homogeneous, two-tier client-server systems with mostly request-response semantics or cluster-based server systems with transactional semantics. These research artifacts most often assume single language and single platform systems, which when incorporated in middleware platforms form point solutions, limit reuse, and are too restrictive for enterprise DRE systems.

Lack of support for mixed-mode dependability semantics. DRE systems of interest to us require mix mode dependability wherein parts of the system may require ultra high availability calling for solutions that require active replication schemes while other parts of the systems may demand passive forms of replication to overcome issues with non-determinism.

Lack of support for variable failover granularity and failure risk management. In enterprise DRE systems, traditional approaches to fault tolerance that rely on replication and recovery of a single server process or a single host are not sufficient since the fault management schemes must now account for the timely and simultaneous failover of groups of entities while also improving the system availability by minimizing the risk of simultaneous failures of groups of replicated entities.

Lack of intuitive and scalable dependability provisioning tools. Standardized middleware solutions to dependability, such as FT-CORBA [2], provide a *one-size-fits-all* approach, which do not support the different properties, such as mixed-mode dependability semantics, required by enterprise DRE systems. Moreover, dependability provisioning in DRE systems tend to use imperative, programmatic mechanisms which are tedious, inflexible, non reusable and error prone, and cannot scale to large enterprise DRE systems, where heterogeneity of the underlying platforms is the norm.

To address the challenges outlined above, design-time tools that can automate the dependability provisioning problem for enterprise DRE systems are needed. This paper describes *MDDPro* (Model Driven Dependability Provisioning), which is a Model-driven Engineering (MDE) [3] tool for design-time dependability provisioning in enterprise DRE systems. We demonstrate

- how the intuitive modeling capabilities in our tool can model fault tolerance elements in DRE systems at different granularities,
- how system availability can be enhanced by applying replica placement decision algorithms on the models, and

- how generative programming capabilities in the tool can be used to rapidly and reliably provision dependability in DRE systems.

The rest of the paper is organized as follows: Section 2 describes the challenges in designing the dependability provisioning tool for enterprise DRE systems; Section 3 describes the design and implementation of our dependability provisioning tool; Section 4 describes related research; and Section 5 provides concluding remarks and directions for future research.

2   Design Considerations for Automated Dependability Provisioning

Several factors must be considered when developing a dependability provisioning tool, such as MDDPro, for enterprise DRE systems. In this section we use a sample enterprise DRE system as a guiding example to outline the requirements of such a design-time tool.

2.1   Enterprise DRE System Case Study

Figure 1 illustrates a sample enterprise DRE system drawn from representative domains, such as avionics mission computing or shipboard computing, where variables of interest are sensed by the sensor equipment, which are software controlled and fed to a set of planners who determine the appropriate control action to be taken, and subsequently relay this information to the actuator software components.

Enterprise DRE systems are often deployed over heterogeneous platforms, which consist of multiple different networks, hardware and several layers of software. We consider the fact that failures may occur in any of these entities. For example, node failures, operating system crashes, middleware broker process failures, and even network link failures are common. In our current discussion we do not consider multiple cascaded failures.

Quite often the critical functionality of enterprise DRE systems is spread across multiple components. For example, the planning activity in Figure 1 is spread across two planning components, which could be deployed in separate application servers on different hosts. Since these distributed set of components form a unit of critical functionality, for high availability and even for the correct

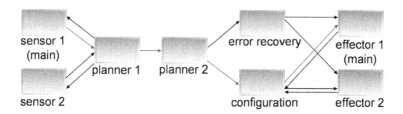

Fig. 1. A Sample Enterprise DRE System

operation of the system, it may be required that all such components in the critical path be protected against failure.

Moreover, if any of these individual components fail, it may not be sufficient to recover only the failed component but rather the failover should recover a group of critical components. This is because failure recovery takes finite amount of time and therefore by the time the failed functionality is recovered, the system may lose some critical system events. Therefore, it is highly desirable in such situations to failover to another replica of the protected group of the components although the failure may occur in only a single component. Thus, the fault recovery granularity can be much larger than the system elements affected by the single failure. The functionality and the topology of replica workflow could be different from that of the primary set of components to account for graceful degradation.

Risk management and availability considerations in enterprise DRE systems involve how individual or groups of critical components are replicated and deployed. Effective deployment of replica (or replica groups) minimize the risk of simultaneous failures in individual replica groups thereby improving the availability of the system.

2.2   Design Considerations

Using the enterprise DRE system case study illustrated in Figure 1 and the dependability management requirements outlined above, we now describe the design considerations for an automated dependability provisioning tool for enterprise DRE systems. In the following we describe the desired characteristics of such a design tool.

1. **Variable granularity of system protection:** Enterprise DRE systems are composed of several independently deployable assemblies of components that communicate together in a workflow fashion to carry out the system's functionality. Quite often the unit of modularity in the system design is larger than a single deployed component and results in some critical functionality of the system being spread across multiple components and/or assemblies. As outlined in the case study, in terms of the availability perspective, the entire critical functionality which is spread across multiple components must now be protected from failures. Moreover, failure of any one component in the workflow now implies the failure of the entire flow. In such a situation, the system must failover to a redundant workflow as opposed to a single component. One strategy for the failover mechanism could be to allow graceful degradation. The functionality of the replica components may not be the exact duplicate of the original. For example, the replica component can possibly implement an algorithm that is less resource hungry compared to the primary.

   A design-time tool must allow the specification of these requirements of enterprise DRE system. Section 3.2 describes how MDDPro provides intuitive abstractions to capture these dependability requirements of enterprise DRE systems.

2. **Mixed-mode dependability requirements:** Enterprise DRE systems are large-scale and comprise several different components each of which accomplishing specific tasks of the entire system functionality. Some parts of the system may require ultra high reliability mandating active replication schemes. However, due to the overhead associated with active replication and the non determinism issues [4, 5] involved in active replication, it may be necessary to restrict the use of active replication to a small part of the enterprise DRE systems. Other parts of the system may then use other forms of replication, such as passive replication, or depend on simple restart mechanisms depending on the criticality of the component and available resources in the system.

   The design-time tool must enable enterprise DRE system developers to capture these mixed-mode dependability semantics of the system. When combined with the granularity of protection units and other performance requirements of the system, this provisioning task becomes complex to perform manually using ad hoc and programmatic techniques. Section 3.2 describes how MDDPro provides intuitive abstractions to capture mixed-mode dependability requirements of enterprise DRE systems.

3. **Effective replica deployment for maximizing availability:** As alluded to above, enterprise DRE systems may have a number of different protected units of functionality that are assembled together to form the system. Moreover, different parts of the system may use different replication schemes. Considering both these requirements, it is now necessary to introduce redundancy in the system that accounts for the units of protection used and the replication styles used. Redundancy in the system improves system availability, however, high levels of reliability are realized only when replicas are placed in such a way that the risk of simultaneous failures of replicas is minimized. Effective replica placement also impacts several other performance characteristics of the entire system. For example, effective replica placement may be necessary to maintain a bounded and fast state synchronization among the replicas.

   A design-time tool can be used to ensure that the system simultaneously satisfies multiple QoS requirements such as performance, predictability and availability, by incorporating deployment state space search algorithms that automatically find effective deployments. This feature boils down to the general problem of constraint satisfaction. Optimality is a harder problem than constraint satisfaction, however, we do not consider it yet in our design. Section 3.3 describes how we have designed our MDDPro tool that can plug in different replica placement algorithms that find effective deployments for enterprise DRE systems.

4. **Automated provisioning of dependability:** Even though the modeling techniques can help capture dependability requirements while replica placement algorithms can provide effective deployment decisions, these must ultimately be realized in the context of the underlying hosting platforms, such as the component middleware. Component middleware often use XML

metadata that describes how components of an enterprise DRE system should be hosted in the middleware and how they must be connected to each other. For large-scale systems, the amount of metadata becomes very large and ad hoc techniques, such as handcrafting these descriptors becomes infeasible and error prone.

Dependability provisioning makes this task harder since the metadata must now account for the protection units and provisioning the multiple replication schemes within the enterprise DRE system. This requires substantial degree of middleware configuration by allocating different resources end-to-end. Replication adds to the number of connections that must be established between the different protection units and their replicas. The replication style makes this task even harder. For example, when active replication is used, the middleware must be configured to use a group communication substrate that is used by the communication between replicas. On the other hand, in passive replication, the secondary replicas must be provisioned on the middleware to accept periodic state updates from the primary. Section 3.4 describes how generative programming [6] techniques used within our MDDPro tool automates the metadata generation to provision dependability for enterprise DRE systems within the middleware platforms.

Solution Approach. Model Driven Engineering (MDE) [3] is a promising approach to provision the dependability requirements for enterprise DRE systems because it raises the level of the abstraction of system design to a level higher than third-generation programming languages by providing a scalable and intuitive abstractions that are closer to the domain. The *model-per-concern* paradigm within MDE alleviates system complexity because it abstracts away the irrelevant details from the developer's current "view" of the system. Generative tools provided by MDE approaches can seamlessly integrate multiple views of the system and produce a consistent set of metadata used by underlying hardware/software platforms for configuration. The MDDPro tool described in this paper is therefore based on the MDE approach.

3   Dependability Provisioning Using Model-Driven Engineering

In this section we describe the design and implementation of our MDDPro design-time, automated dependability provisioning tool, which uses a model-driven engineering (MDE) approach in its design and satisfies the requirements of such a tool outlined in Section 2.2.

3.1   Overview of Enabling Technologies

Before delving into the details of our design-time dependability provisioning tool, we first provide an overview of the enabling technologies we have leveraged to develop MDDPro.

MDDPro has been developed in the context of the CoSMIC (Component Synthesis with Model Integrated Computing) [7] MDE toolsuite. CoSMIC is an open source MDE tool suite used to simplify the development of component-based DRE applications focusing particularly on the assembly, deployment, configuration, and validation of component-based enterprise DRE systems. CoSMIC comprises a collection of *domain-specific modeling languages* (DSMLs), which define the concepts, relationships, and constraints used to express domain entities [8], and generative programming capabilities that automate the different development concerns of DRE systems.

The different capabilities in CoSMIC including the MDDPro tool described in this paper have been developed using the Generic Modeling Environment (GME) [9]. GME is a metaprogrammable modeling environment that enables domain experts to develop visual modeling languages and generative tools associated with those languages. The modeling languages in GME are represented as metamodels. A metamodel in GME depicts a class diagram using UML-like constructs showcasing the elements of the modeling language and how they are associated with each other.

A key CoSMIC DSML developed in GME is the *Platform Independent Component Modeling Language* (PICML) [10], which enables graphical manipulation of modeling elements, such as component ports and attributes. PICML also performs various types of generative actions, such as synthesizing XML-based deployment plan descriptors defined in the OMG Deployment and Configuration (D&C) specification [11]. CoSMIC provides the *Component QoS Modeling Language* (CQML), which is a mapping of the platform-independent PICML models to models that are specific to the lightweight CORBA Component Model. Figure 2 illustrates the CQML model for the enterprise DRE system case study from Figure 1. Our MDDPro tool is an enhancement to the CQML DSML and its generative capabilities.

3.2   Modeling Dependability Requirements in MDDPro

We now describe how the MDDPro tool addresses Requirements (1) and (2) described in Section 2.2. CQML allows modelers to annotate the system elements modeled with platform-specific details and different quality of service (QoS) requirements as shown in Figure 2. MDDPro is responsible for the dependability QoS attributes in CQML. The artifacts that can be annotated are component instances, component implementations, connections between component ports, component assemblies, among others.

MDDPro allows an enterprise DRE system deployer to model the dependability requirements in the QoS view of the DRE system as shown in Figure 3. The QoS view leverages the basic structure of the DRE system in terms of the component instances in an assembly, component ports and their inter connections. It allows FT elements to be modeled orthogonally to the system components and therefore achieves separation of dependability concerns from the primary system composition and functionality concerns.

The following modeling elements are supported within MDDPro:

- **Failover units (FOUs),** which enable control over the granularity of protected system components, such as software components, component assemblies, or entire component workflows. Failure of any one element belonging to a FOU is treated equivalent to the failure of all the elements in the FOU and the system effectively "fails over" to another replica of the FOU. This modeling abstraction not only captures the failover granularities of system entities, but also the degree of replication for each FOU and other systemic requirements, such as the periodicity of liveness monitoring for FOUs. The degree of replication is represented as a pair of numbers representing minimum and maximum number of replicas. The programming language artifacts that implement the replica components could be different from that of the primary components allowing graceful degradation of the functionality if the dependability solution desires it.

  Frequently, the liveness of distributed components is monitored using a "heart beat" protocol. The frequency of the heartbeat is one configurable parameter in the liveness monitoring, which can be configured in MDDPro. The heartbeat itself is configurable in two ways: *push model* or *pull model*. Thus, the directionality of the heartbeat can also be configured in MDDPro. In Section 3.4 we show how modeling of FOUs enable us to automatically synthesize and configure liveness monitoring components as well as heartbeat producing components. Conceptually, a FOU is an abstraction to capture the availability requirements at the control plane of the dependability solution.

- **Replication groups (RGs),** which allows capturing the replication requirements of software components within a FOU. These models specify replication strategies, such as active, passive or other variants, and the state synchronization policies for components. A replication group captures the

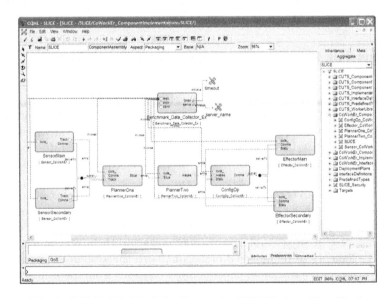

Fig. 2. CQML Model of the Enterprise DRE System Case Study

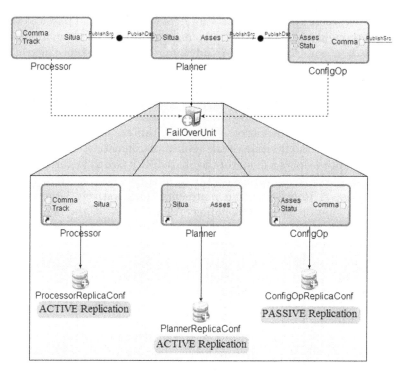

Fig. 3. Availability Requirements Modeling in CQML

configuration parameters related to the data plane of the deployment solution. Multiple replicas of the system components synchronize their state
with each other as per the configuration of the data plane. For example,
data synchronization frequency of the replicas is configurable. Moreover, the
topology of state synchronization among replicas is also a data plane level
configuration issue handled in MDDPro.

- **Shared Risk Groups (SRGs),** which defines one way of grouping of the
  resources in the target network of the applications that share a risk of simultaneous failure. Application components share a risk of simultaneous failure
  by virtue of the failure of the resources they share, such as processes, nodes,
  racks or even data centers on which they are hosted. Risk factors are determined by assigning the metrics, such as co-failure probabilities to a hierarchy
  of the network resources in a risk group that affects the availability of the
  system. The computation of the co-failure probabilities themselves is beyond
  the scope of this paper and is assumed to be done apriori using reliability
  engineering methodologies.

  The primary purpose behind modeling the shared risk groups and their
  respective co-failure probabilities is to facilitate automated deployment decisions of the components in the system such that the probability of failure of
  entire system is minimized thereby increasing the availability. One way of reducing the co-failure probability is to increase the physical distance between

the nodes where the components are deployed. Here, the physical distance can be thought of as the distance from a remote host or a remote blade or a remote data center and so on. An advantage of using distance metric is that it is simpler and quite intuitive than co-failure probability. In Section 3.3 we show how the shared risk group model is used by the MDDPro model interpreter to determine a suitable and effective deployment that satisfies the availability requirements and minimizes risks of simultaneous failures. In our prototype implementation of the algorithm we use the simpler distance metric to guide the decision of the replica placement.

The Figure 4 shows a model of the Shared Risk Group hierarchy. Hosts 1 to 5 are part of a domain and are contained under a common "RootRiskGroup" at the top. A RootRiskGroup represents comparatively larger structures such as a ship or an entire building. All the hosts in the domain share a common risk of failure of the largest composing structure represented by a RootRiskGroup. We limit the scope of our dependability solution at that level. The RootRiskGroup is further divided in to smaller units of Shared Risk Groups as shown in the figure. For example, Host1, Host4 and Host5 share a common risk of a failure of the NodeGroup1 but failure of Node-Group2 that consists of Host4 and Host 5 does not affect Host1.

The distance between hosts is simply computed as the number of tree edges between two hosts. For example, the distance between the Host2 and Host3 is 2. Similarly the distance between the Host2 and the Host4 or Host5 is 5. Based on such a Shared Risk Group hierarchy, deployment decisions are taken to maximize the distance between the primary component and its replicas as shown in the Figure 4.

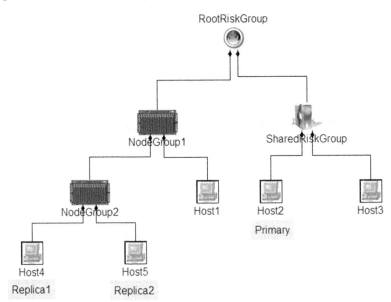

Fig. 4. Shared Risk Group Hierarchy Modeling in CQML

3.3   Improving Availability Via Effective Replica Placement

Requirement (3) in Section 2.2 states that the dependability solution for enterprise DRE systems must minimize the risk of simultaneous failures of replicated functionality. This requires effective replica placement algorithms, where replication is provided for protection units that are modeled as failover units described in Section 3.2.

MDDPro uses GME's plugin capabilities to add model interpreters. One such model interpreter addresses the replica placement problem. The placement model interpreter provides a strategizable framework that can use different constraint-based algorithms to determine an effective replica placement plan to minimize the co-failure probability of the system as a whole.

Formulation of replica placement problem instance in MDDPro. In one instantiation of the formulation of the replica placement problem within our strategizable model interpreter, we use mathematical vectors to represent the distance of the replicas from the primary component. If the primary component has N replicas, then we form N orthogonal vectors, where each vector represents the distance from the primary component node in terms of hops captured in the shared risk group hierarchy. The magnitude of the resultant vector of the N orthogonal vectors is used to compare different deployment configurations and to find the one that satisfies the constraints.

In this formulation of the placement problem algorithm, we have taken care to avoid generation of some obviously undesirable deployment configurations of the system. For example, it does not allow deployment configuration where all the replicas of a component are located in the same host. This is obviously undesirable in dependable enterprise DRE systems because placing multiple replicas in the same host increases the risk of simultaneous failure of replicas.

Prototype heuristic algorithm using the distance metric. The prototype placement algorithm that we have developed maximizes the distance of the replicas from the primary replica but the pair-wise distance between replicas themselves can be small. In other words, the replicas themselves can group together in closely located hosts that are farthest from the primary host. Such a deployment configuration is skewed and undesirable. To alleviate the problem we apply a penalty function to the resultant magnitude of the vector. The penalty function gives more precedence to uniform deployments than highly skewed deployments. The penalty function that we have used is a simple standard deviation of the distances of individual replicas from the primary component. We can generate better configurations by penalizing highly skewed deployment configurations heavily compared to the more uniform deployment configurations.

For example, consider two resultant vectors $v1\{4,4,4\}$ and $v2\{1,1,8\}$ having 3 dimensions. Although the magnitude of v2 is much greater than v1, the deployment configuration captured in v1 is more desirable than v2 because the replicas are spread across more uniformly around the primary unlike v2. The heuristic algorithm for the prototype implementation of the deployment algorithm is illustrated in Listing 1.

```
1. Compute the distance from each of the replicas to the primary for a placement.

2. Record each distance as a vector, where all vectors are orthogonal.

3. Add the vectors to obtain a resultant.

4. Compute the magnitude of the resultant.

5. Use the resultant in all comparisons (either among placements or against a threshold)

6. Apply a penalty function to the composite distance (e.g. pairwise replica distance)
```

Listing 1: Replica Placement Heuristics

3.4   Automated Dependability Provisioning Via Generative Programming

The model interpreters and generative tools in MDDPro use the dependability requirements captured in the models for synthesizing metadata used to provision dependability for enterprise DRE systems. In order to realize such an automation in the provisioning process several artifacts of dependability must be addressed: (a) the designer of the dependable system has to annotate the desired degree of replication of the protected components in the model, (b) the generative tools have to process the replication requirements and produce deployment metadata that reflects the number of physical software components that will actually be deployed but not necessarily be represented in the model, (c) derive the complex connection topology interconnecting the generated components, which is dictated by the degree and style of replication of the primary component as well as replication requirements of the components it interacts with, and (d) generating the fault-tolerance infrastructure components that produce a periodic heartbeat as well as monitor the liveness of the replicated components.

Deployment metadata generation framework. As noted in Section 3.1, the real-time component middleware platforms used to host the enterprise DRE systems use standardized XML-based metadata descriptors to describe the deployment plans of the entire system, which the runtime system uses to actually deploy the different components of the system. Our challenge involved enhancing the metadata descriptors to include dependability provisioning decisions. For this goal to realize, MDDPro's generative capabilities had to be integrated with the existing generators available in CQML without obtrusive changes to existing capabilities. This approach ensures that generators for QoS issues beyond dependability, such as security, can seamlessly be integrated with CQML.

   To address these concerns, we have developed an extensible framework called *The Deployment Plan Framework* that allows augmentation of metadata generation "on-the-fly" as it is being generated. The framework exposes a fixed set of hooks to be filled in by the developer of the existing and any new CQML model interpreters including the MDDPro model interpreters. The main job of the deployment framework is to generate the standardized metadata describing the components, their implementations, their inter-connections and so on. Additionally, it invokes predefined hook methods implemented by different QoS model interpreters of CQML. The MDDPro interpreter implements a subset of a large set of different possible hook methods. The hook methods "inject" auto-generated standardized metadata in response to the availability requirements captured in the model. The metadata generated on-the-fly blends into the other standardized metadata.

This architecture allows large scale reuse of earlier code base that deals with the basic structure and composition capabilities of PICML/CQML. The developer producing QoS enhancements to the existing modeling capabilities of CQML need not be concerned with the other complexity of the framework and the format of the standardized descriptors, but simply add/modify the metadata for the QoS dimension they are addressing. Our MDDPro model interpreter exploits these capabilities of the Deployment Plan Framework to "inject" three different kinds of metadata.

1. **Replica component instances** of the primary protected component depending upon replication degree annotated in the model. For example, if replication degree of an FOU is 3, then two replicas of the primary FOU are created. Thus, two replicas of each component in the FOU are effectively added by the interpreter.

2. **Component connection metadata** is injected based on the replication style and degree of replication. The incoming connections to the protected components are marked with special annotations so that the run-time system can use suitable implementations to realize them. One such possible annotation is IOGR, i.e. Interoperable Object Group Reference. IOGR is a part of the FT-CORBA [2] standard.

3. **Deployment metadata** is the assignment of components to computing resources available in the system. This metadata includes information for all the primary protected components, their replicas and the dependability infrastructure components (e.g. Heartbeat components).

Handling complex connections. As shown in Figure 5, shows the effect of the replication style and the degree of replication on the complexity of the connection establishment. In an unprotected system, the Processor component and the Planner component have exactly one connection between them. The Figure 5 captures the multiplicative increase in the number of connections when both, the Processor component and the Planner component, are protected using active replication. Each Processor component, primary as well as its replica has to make three connections to each member of the Planner replica group because the degree of replication of the Planner fail over unit (FOU) is three. In general, if the source component of the connection is replicated M times and the destination component is replicated N times then the number of connections grow by a factor of M x N.

Note that the diagram only indicates the necessary number of connections the middleware has to establish when components are deployed. These connection

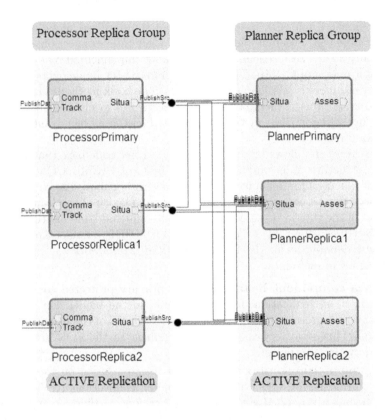

Fig. 5. Complexity of connection generation

may or may not actually be used to send requests across because it really depends upon where request/reply suppression is in place. Nevertheless, the component container has to prepare for any unforeseen failures and has to establish connections *apriori* in order to avoid the latency of connection establishment later when failures occur. The model interpreter that we have developed completely hides away the complexity of modeling the component replica instances and the connections between them.

Automatic generation of liveness monitoring infrastructure. The model interpreter also generates the infrastructure components necessary for liveness monitoring of the protected components. It uses the availability requirements in the models to generate supporting run-time components to realize ready-to-deploy, robust, and fault-tolerant enterprise DRE systems. This includes generating, configuring, and deploying the status monitoring and fault recovery components without the need for the application developer having to model/develop them explicitly.

The generated architecture shown in Figure 6 has two important components: the heartbeat (HB) component and the Fault Protection Center component (FPC).

The purpose of the HB components is to send a periodic heartbeat beacon to the FPC or respond to the periodic liveness poll request received from the FPC. The FPC is the central controlling component that ensures the liveness of the protected components using either pull or push model of the heartbeat beacon. The HB components are collocated with the protected components. The underlying assumption is that the HB component and the protected component would fail simultaneously in the face of a failure. The central FPC component is also replicated to avoid single point of failure. Multiple copies of the FPC components send heartbeat beacons among themselves to ensure that FPC themselves are alive and are doing continuous liveness monitoring of the system.

As shown in Figure 6, every protected component has its own collocated HB component and there is one FPC for every FOU. All the HB components belonging to one FOU send heartbeat to its corresponding FPC. Multiple simultaneously active FOUs have equal number of FPCs, which communicate with themselves to prevent single point of failure.

The heartbeat frequency at which the liveness indications are sent between HBs and FPCs is configurable in the model. The advantage of this architecture is that the infrastructure components for liveness monitoring can be auto-generated using generative technologies. The necessary deployment metadata required to collocate the HB components with their respective protected components and to establish the connections between HB components and the FPC components is auto-generated by the model interpreter from the requirements. Moreover, the metadata that captures the configuration of HB components such as push/pull model and heartbeat frequency is auto-generated for every HB component.

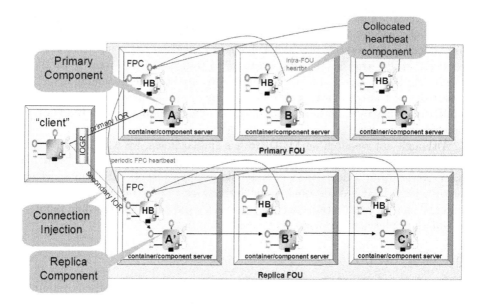

Fig. 6. Generated Deployment of Dependability Infrastructure Elements

4 Related Work

Although there has been substantial research in dependability mechanisms and algorithms over the past several decades, applying modeling and generative techniques to automate dependability provisioning has recently caught researchers' attention. In this section we compare our work on model-driven engineering of dependability with related research.

The CORRECT [12] project describes a project that is looking at applying step-wise refinement and OMG's Model Driven Architecture [13] to automatically generate Java code used in a fault tolerant distributed system. The project uses UML to describe the software architecture in both a platform-independent and platform-specific form. Model-to-model transformations are used to incrementally enrich the models with platform-specific artifacts until the Java skeleton code is generated. MDDPro, on the other hand, is designed to automatically generate the complete source code (not just the skeletons) for the component liveness monitoring infrastructure that detects exceptional conditions.

The research on software systems reliability using MDA [14] focuses on a platform-independent means to support reliability design following the principles of a model driven architecture and approach. The research aims to systematically address dependability concerns from the early to the late stages of software development by expressing dependability architectures using profiles. Design profiles are mapped to deployment domains, where the reliability configurations of how the components communicate and are distributed is explained. Unlike the previous approach, MDDPro uses an extensible way to automatically generate platform specific metadata and programming language artifacts that realize parts of the dependability provisioning solution.

UML has been used perform model-driven dependability analysis [15] for composite web services. The UML representation is based on BPEL, and extensions are added to characterize the fault behavior of the elements comprising the web services. Model transformations are used to map the UML models to Block Diagrams, Fault Trees and Markov models to analyze the dependability characteristics of the composite web services. On the other hand, our approach in MDDPro enhances the productivity of the system developers rather than system dependability analysts.

Although our research on MDDPro has similar goals, we use the concept of domain-specific modeling languages, which provides more richer and semantically powerful modeling concepts than the general-purpose modeling elements provided by UML. Additionally our framework allows plugging in multiple different model interpreters that can synthesize metadata for multiple different middleware platforms provide deployment planning.

5 Conclusions

This paper describes how model driven engineering (MDE) can be used to simplify and automate dependability provisioning in enterprise distributed real-time and embedded (DRE) systems. We describe the capabilities of the MDDPro

(Model Driven Dependability Provisioning) MDE tool which we have built as part of the CoSMIC tool suite. Our work is suitable for component-oriented systems that have multiple different quality of service requirements and which are deployed and configured via declarative mechanisms. Both these traits are common to systems that use the service oriented architecture. In the remainder of this section we describe the lessons we learned in this effort and our future work in this realm.

Lessons Learned and Future Work

Capturing availability requirements in terms of degree of replication, replication style at the modeling time and generating component infrastructure components increases productivity to a great extent but many unresolved challenges still remain.

- **Availability model analysis** is useful to determine the effect of the availability requirements on other QoS aspects of the system. Our prototype implementation of MDDPro is simplistic because it neglects the effects on system resource consumption due to replication. Unconstrained increase in the degree of replication of the protected components in the system may result in excessive resource consumption and may adversely affect other QoS guarantees of the system such as timeliness and CPU load. An analysis technique needs to be in place that would help the system designers take correct decisions about the system availability without adversely affecting the resource consumption and other QoS characteristics of the system.

- **Run-time adaptation** of the fault-tolerance infrastructure as well as the replicated application components is highly desirable in enterprise DRE systems because these systems usually exhibit modal behavior. System functionality as well QoS priorities may change as the mode of operation of the system changes. Our approach to the availability modeling is static in nature and depends on the availability of the target domain information and their associations with each other in terms of co-failure probability. Although the placement model interpreter does take deployment decisions at design time using a strategizable constraint-solver framework, it does not make the system adaptive at run-time. Runtime monitoring subsystems such as RACE can be used to implement a general purpose resource constraint-solver framework at runtime, not unlike the one we have in our design-time placement model interpreter. Such a framework would make intelligent (re)deployment decisions based on changing environment (failures, resource consumption) and modes of the eDRE systems.

- **Ensuring state consistency** across replicas of components or FOUs in a general is a challenge. Our availability model abstracts away the details of the fault monitoring part of the FT subsystem and generates component based infrastructure automatically for precisely doing that. However, state synchronization and ensuring state consistency across replicated components of the system is a hard problem. The primary challenges in this space are capturing and provisioning a variety of state synchronization mechanisms because different component developers may implement different mechanisms as they see fit. Several different ways of ensuring state synchronization are used, for example, central repository/database-based approach, transmission of periodic state updates using point-to-point communication or multicast communication. Modeling the topology transmission of state update messages is also important in case of non repository-based techniques because the runtime failover critically depends on the order in which replica components receive state updates.

All artifacts described in this paper are available in open source from the CoSMIC web site (www.dre.vanderbilt.edu/cosmic).

References

1. Object Management Group: Lightweight CCM FTF Convenience Document. ptc/04-06-10 edn. (June 2004)
2. Object Management Group: Fault Tolerant CORBA Specification. OMG Document orbos/99-12-08 edn. (December 1999)
3. Schmidt, D.C.: Model-Driven Engineering. IEEE Computer **39**(2) (2006) 25–31
4. Pascal Felber and Priya Narasimhan: Experiences, Approaches and Challenges in building Fault-tolerant CORBA Systems. Transactions of Computers **54**(5) (May 2004) 497–511
5. Priya Narasimhan and Tudor Dumitras and Aaron M. Paulos and Soila M. Pertet and Charlie F. Reverte and Joseph G. Slember and Deepti Srivastava: MEAD: support for Real-Time Fault-Tolerant CORBA. Concurrency - Practice and Experience **17**(12) (2005) 1527–1545
6. Czarnecki, K., Eisenecker, U.W.: Generative Programming: Methods, Tools, and Applications. Addison-Wesley, Reading, Massachusetts (2000)
7. Gokhale, A., Schmidt, D.C., Natarajan, B., Gray, J., Wang, N.: Model Driven Middleware. In Mahmoud, Q., ed.: Middleware for Communications. Wiley and Sons, New York (2004) 163–187
8. Karsai, G., Sztipanovits, J., Ledeczi, A., Bapty, T.: Model-Integrated Development of Embedded Software. Proceedings of the IEEE **91**(1) (January 2003) 145–164
9. Ledeczi, A., Bakay, A., Maroti, M., Volgysei, P., Nordstrom, G., Sprinkle, J., Karsai, G.: Composing Domain-Specific Design Environments. IEEE Computer (November 2001) 44–51
10. Balasubramanian, K., Balasubramanian, J., Parsons, J., Gokhale, A., Schmidt, D.C.: A Platform-Independent Component Modeling Language for Distributed Real-time and Embedded Systems. Elsevier Journal of Computer and System Sciences (2006) 171–185
11. Object Management Group: Deployment and Configuration Adopted Submission. OMG Document mars/03-05-08 edn. (July 2003)
12. Capozucca, A., Gallina, B., Guelfi, N., Pelliccione, P., Romanovsky, A.: CORRECT - Developing Fault-Tolerant Distributed Systems. ERCIM News **64**(1) (2006)
13. Object Management Group: Model Driven Architecture (MDA). OMG Document ormsc/2001-07-01 edn. (July 2001)
14. G.Rodrigues: A Model Driven Approach for Software Systems Reliability. In: In the proceedings of the 26th ICSE/Doctoral Symposium, May 2004 - Edinburgh, Scotland, ACM Press (May 2004)
15. Zarras, A., Vassiliadis, P., Issarny, V.: Model-Driven Dependability Analysis of Web Services. In: Proc. of the Intl. Symp. on Dist. Objects and Applications (DOA'04), Agia Napa, Cyprus (October 2004)

Applying US DoD Human Engineering Methods to Reduce Procedural Error Related Outages

Pat O'Brien

Reliability and Availability
Motorola, Embedded Communications Computing
214-882-1049
epob@obrienbusdev.com, Harry.Weber@motorola.com

Abstract. Human errors committed by network equipment (NE) maintainers cause the largest portion of all network outages and down time. This paper describes the application of US Department of Defense Human Engineering methods to resolve conflicts in standards; and, to identify and remove the root causes of design induced procedural errors. It demonstrates the application of human Fault Mode and Effects Analysis in the design of Motorola's AdvancedTCA® equipment. It also shows the resulting feedback loop to engineers to change the human-machine interface. The paper gives examples of reduced procedural error rates expected to result from the changes in the interface design.

Keywords: Human Factors Engineering, Procedural Errors, Interface Design, Usability, Man-Machine Interaction.

1 Situation

Motorola intends to field a superior AdvancedTCA® (ATCA®) platform. Initial concerns were to ensure the desired functionality was present in the network equipment (NE). The industry and Motorola succeeded at this and support a wide range of high volume broadband voice, data and other communication applications. With this accomplished secondary concerns of reducing lifecycle costs and achieving 6NINES (99.9999%) availability have come to the forefront.

Lifecycle costs and availability depend upon maintenance induced costs and down time. Theoretically, equipment could be so reliable that it simply would not fail, thus, maintenance related outages and costs would drop to zero. Ten years ago, some logisticians explored how far this notion could be taken and designed supply chain models based upon an assumption that UPS, DHL and other delivery drivers would maintain the physical system. The equipment would be so simple to maintain that the logistics/delivery drivers would have a key to the equipment room, would find the physical address of parts and would, themselves, replace the parts.

Unfortunately, such notions remain unrealistic for the most part. Rather, maintenance remains a critical component of keeping systems running. Additionally, the increasing complexity of NE has resulted in increasingly complex procedures. Procedural errors account for nearly 50% of network outages with the range across

M. Malek et al.(Eds.): ISAS 2007, LNCS 4526, pp. 145–154, 2007.
© Springer-Verlag Berlin Heidelberg 2007

network operators being from 30 to 60%, based upon analysis of Automated Reporting Management Information System data.

Multiple standards have tried to define the human-machine interfaces to reduce procedural errors. Relying on these standards does not, however, necessarily reduce procedural errors. The standards are incomplete and impose conflicting requirements for the human interface both within and across standards. The PCI Industrial Computer Manufacturers Group (PICMG®) standards guiding the design of NE are a notable example. PICMG is a permissive standard and allows a broad range of "user definable" parameters. Thus, manufacturers are able to design components with advantages over their competitors' products. However, so many parameters are undefined that one can follow PICMG and still have an unusable, error inducing interface.

For example, throughout its standards, PICMG specifies 9pt Arial typeface but then does not leave adequate space in the designated indicator areas of faceplates to place three 9pt Arial characters. Allowing for three characters is important because the shortest romance language abbreviations in an open-ended abbreviation set must be a minimum of three characters long to prevent confusion. Thus, designers are forced to use symbols, transilluminated indicators, alternate type faces and other solutions that are not addressed by the standard.

This lack of precision in the PICMG standards requires some means for filling the gaps and creating integrated, consistent interfaces. Interestingly, turning to other national, international and commercial best practices and standards (i.e., ANSI, ISO, OSHA, Mil-Std, GR-78-CORE, GR-2914-CORE, etc.) can increase conflicts in requirements. An example of conflicts across standards for the simple matter of LED colors is shown in Table 1. The table lists colors PICMG says should be supported and the range of colors specified by various standards.

Such minor deviations when distributed across all the NE in an equipment room results in procedural errors. One vendor's 'green' LED placed next to another vendor's 'green' LED is perceived as being 'yellow'; a 'yellow' LED placed next to

Table 1. Color Specification Conflicts Among Common Standards

PICMG*	ANSI***	ANSI (range)	Mil-Std**	NASA
Blue	470nm	445-480nm	Not used	Not used
Green	525nm	505-535nm	555nm	520nm
Yellow	590nm	583-593nm	575nm	~570nm
Orange	Not used	Not used	585nm	Not defined
Red	630nm	615-650nm	660nm	~635nm

   * PICMG says these colors shall be supported
   ** ANSI 40-2003 and ANSI Z535.1 conflict. 40-2003 does not support an Orange LED definition but ANSI
     Z535.1 supports Orange labeling and signs.
   *** Note that ANSI 'Yellow' is redder than Mil-Std 'Orange'

another vendor's 'amber' LED appears 'green'; an 'amber' LED placed next to another vendor's 'yellow' LED appears 'red'.

Managing superficial interface design features is only part of reducing procedural errors. Incomplete and conflicting standards are compounded by engineers' limited understanding of human engineering. Furthermore, an engineer's practical experience often conflicts with the characteristics of the maintainer population. Most designers have also never had to use their interfaces under actual field conditions and scenarios. This results in errors in the superficial design of the interface due to faulty assumptions about network operations, real world scenarios; and, the physical capabilities, knowledge, training and experience of maintainers. Examples of some problems identified are shown in Table 2. The range of areas the problems can potentially impact is assessed across the Human System Integration domains shown in Table 3.

2 Problem

The problem was how to reduce procedural errors when the root cause was not in the written procedures themselves but rather in the standards or platform design. Equipment design features were found to induce errors or lead to work-arounds that damaged equipment. Also, some engineers mistakenly believed that because they met all the "shalls" or mandatory requirements in PICMG standards, they had achieved a useable interface with low probability of a human error. It is actually more the case that to allow innovation, the standards needed to be somewhat incomplete and the engineers needed to close the gaps themselves. Finally, the actual field data indicated that the interfaces and procedures are designed poorly. This was indicated by both the Automated Reporting Management Information System data that 50% of all downtime is caused by procedural errors; and, by customer anecdotal reports of problems and repair times well beyond what was expected based upon experience with the equipment in the lab.

3 Solution

Given the industry average of 50% downtime being caused by procedural errors Motorola and its customers determined to make a major reduction in this figure. The solution selected was to implement best practices in Human Engineering (HE). The method selected was Mil-HDBK-46855A Human Engineering Program Process and Procedures.

The aspiration was to comply to all PICMG and Telcordia human factors requirements where specified and to use other best practices such as ISO 4192, the FAA-HFDS-001, NASA-STD-3000 and other human engineering design standards and methods to resolve conflicts in PICMG and Telcordia requirements or to fill missing requirements. The solution required not only adherence to standards but also basic research using ethnography, motion-time studies, human Fault Mode and

Table 2. Example Human–machine Interface Design Problems and Impact on Availability and Lifecycle Costs

Feature	Related Standards	Problem	Impact
LEDs	PICMG 3.0 Base Specification GR-78-CORE, GR-2914-CORE, ANSI 40-2003, Mil-Std-759B	LED colors are not specified, resulting in multiple, different and confusing colors being used for Yellow, Green, Amber, Red, etc.	Confusing one color for another leads to incorrect maintainer actions.
LED semantics	PICMG 3.0 Base Specification, GR-2914-CORE, NASA-STD-3000	PICMG LED semantics use 3 LEDs to diagnose 3 states rather than the 8 possible and wastefully use Red and Green LEDs to indicate opposite states in violation of best practices such as NASA-STD-3000	Maintainers do not have adequate diagnostic feedback from the LEDs causing them to seek consoles unnecessarily, hammer on faceplates, break ejectors handles and H/S switches etc in a cascade of trial-and-error attempts to determine FRU states.
Blade ejector handles	PICMG 3.0 Base Specification, GR-2914-CORE, Mil-Std-1472F	The mechanical advantage of handle design is not adequate for 5th percentile females to apply the insertion and extraction forces for FRUs allowed by PICMG and Telcordia	Females ask males to insert some blades, leading to sub-optimal man-power management costs. Alternatively, maintainers break handles, bend faceplates, hammer on faceplates, pull on handles with pliers and use other harmful means to insert and eject FRUs
Shelf "A" side – "B" side confusion	PICMG 3.0 Base Specification, GR-2914-CORE	Engineers reversed the labeling and wiring from front of the chassis to the rear in contradiction to typical industry conventions.	This caused maintainers to disconnect the wrong source of input power during maintenance procedures on chassis operating in a simplex power mode. The result was a total power outage to the chassis.
Chassis finish	PICMG 3.0 Base Specification, NEBs and GR-68-CORE	Requirements for a durable finish caused engineers to use burnished metal. The glare washed out LED, caused reflections and other visual noise that made LEDs not visible from certain angles and distances.	Maintainers stopped relying on LEDs and other visual cues for feedback and resorted to trial-and-error 'hammering' on parts to get them to illuminate.
LED and light pipe shielding	PICMG 3.0, GR-2914-CORE and Mil-Std	Unshielded LEDs/light pipes allowed subtractive color mixing and distortion of LED colors. The state of LEDs could not be trusted.	Maintainers couldn't tell the LED state and stopped using LEDs, preferring to pound on faceplates to get units to 'work'.

Table 3. Human Systems Integration Domains, Mil-Hdbk-46855

Human Engineering	Manpower	Personnel	Training	Safety	Health Hazards	Human Survivability
Effects of design on skill, knowledge and aptitudes, and physical capabilities requirements Compatibility of design with anthropometric and biomedical criteria for the target population Design-driven human performance reliability, effectiveness, efficiency and safety performance requirements Simplicity of operation, maintenance and support Cost of design-driven human error, inefficiency or ineffectiveness Workload, situational awareness and human performance reliability	Manpower requirements Deployment considerations Organizational structure Operating strength Manning concepts Manpower policies	Personnel selection and classification Demographics Accession rates Attrition rates Career progression and retention rates Promotion flow Personnel and training pipeline flow Qualified personnel where and when needed Projected user population recruiting Cognitive, physical and educational profiles	Training concepts and strategy Training tasks and training development methods Media, equipment and facilities Simulation Operational tempo Training system suitability, effectiveness, efficiency and costs Concurrency of system with trainers	Safety of design and procedures under deployed conditions Human error Total system reliability and fault reduction Total system risk reduction	Health hazards induced by systems, environment or task requirements Areas of special interest include but not limited to: • Acoustics • Chemical substances • Radiation • Oxygen deficiency and air pressure • Temperature extremes • Shock and vibration • Laser protection	Threats in the environment Potential injury to personnel Protective equipment Medical injury Fatigue and stress

Effects Analysis and other methods to identify root causes of errors. A sample of human engineering activities performed in this effort contains:

- Mission and scenario analysis
- Task analysis and cognitive task analysis
- Functional flow diagramming
- Decision-action diagramming
- Link analysis
- Motion-time study
- Fault Mode and Effects Analysis

The result of these activities was publication of multiple human engineering design reviews and studies; and requests submitted to a Change Control Board to change the product design.

4 Problems and Solutions

Executing the design reviews against standards, performing motion-time studies and ethnographic studies with customer craftspersons, conducting contextual inquiry and talk-aloud protocol analysis, and using other methods on site with customers and in our labs identified multiple sources of procedural errors. Some examples of these and their solutions follow.

Port-Starboard Versus Read Right-to-Left

Designers had a choice between two conventions for labeling the front and back of an equipment chassis. The PICMG standard did not specify a convention. The initial design selected was to use a convention of labeling FRUs from left to right with "1" or "A" on the left and following markings increasing to the right on both the front and the back of the equipment. The two options are shown in Figure 1. During usability testing of the power entry module (PEM) replacement procedure, a test subject mistakenly cut power to the simplex power on PEM, this resulted in a total loss of power to the chassis. The root cause was essentially confusion between which circuit breaker at an input power source went to which PEM. Upon investigating maintainers' mental models of the equipment, it was judged that fewer such mistakes would be associated with the "port-starboard" convention rather than using a "left-to-right" convention. Figure 2 shows the probabilities of a maintainer making the mistake of cutting the wrong pair of two adjacent circuit breakers when the PEM labeling and wiring is reversed.

As seen from Figure 2 and based upon judgment based on experience and Nuclear Regulatory Commission data, there is a relatively high probability of a total shelf outage occurring when using a "read left-to-right" convention rather than the normal

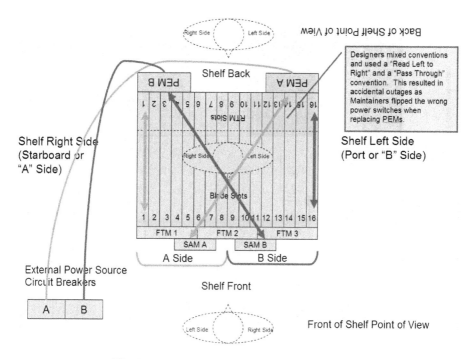

Fig. 1. Two Optional Metaphors for Chassis Labeling

'port-starboard". The initial "read left-to-right" design was estimated to result in an outage during 18% of all PEM replacement procedures, or p = .18. The "port-starboard" convention was estimated to result in an outage three times in one thousand, p = .003.

Glare and Color Distortion

Motorola engineers preferred a burnished metal finish to meet durability requirements. This created a high glare surface that caused multiple reflections and "visual noise". In the case of critical indicators embedded in a field of noise, maintainers learn to ignore points of light, including meaningful LEDs through a process called "habituation". Additionally, Figure 3 shows unshielded LEDs and light pipes. These caused some indicators to appear illuminated when they are not illuminated and distort the colors of other indicators.

In a visually noisy environment, the human is unreliable because the signals are not reliably perceived and can be confused or ignored as part of the background noise. As seen in Figure 3, there are multiple sources of reflected light, false indications and color distortions that create visual noise. Such distortions can trigger the maintainer to take an incorrect action or fail to respond to a spot of color the brain has learned to ignore. Change requests to put a matte gray finish on the equipment and to shield LEDs and light pipes were submitted and accepted.

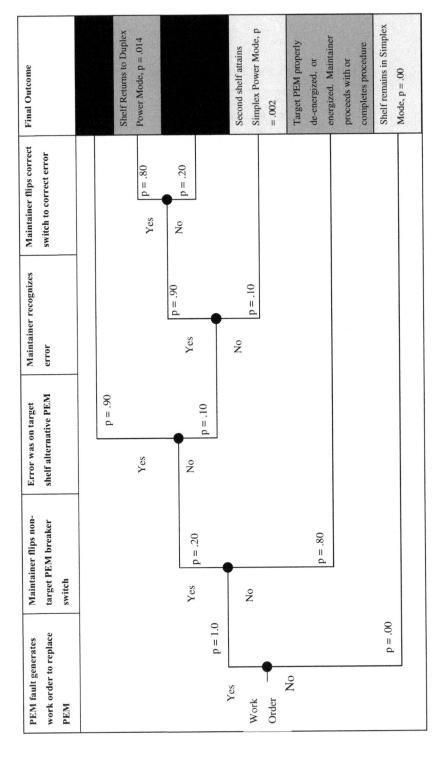

Fig. 2. Reversed Labeling to Circuit Breaker Event Tree, Probability Estimated from NUREG/CR-1278: Handbook of Human Reliability Analysis

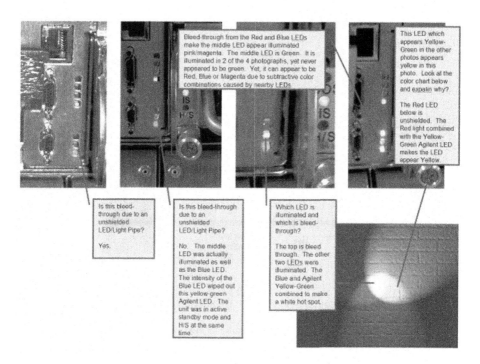

Fig. 3. Color Distortions, Reflections and False Indications

Faceplate Layout and Label Orientation

Faceplates are a major part of the human-machine interface. While the industry aspires to allocate all interaction with equipment to a development environment, the reality is that many applications and customers' logistics and maintenance philosophies continue to require substantial amounts of information to be conveyed to maintainers through the faceplate of the equipment rather than a console. Faceplate design, thus, remains a source of human error.

Faceplate design can be a complex problem involving the task sequences and information needs of the operator/maintainer as they execute critical scenarios. The design involves clustering information into an architecture that makes the most critical information for a scenario highly noticeable. Even mistakes made at a superficial level can, however, drive a human to respond to the information provided incorrectly. Simple errors that designers made involved violations in the orientation of labels and violation of the Laws of Pragnanz, which are rules that govern how mental processes cluster information into meaningful groups of information. Figure 4 shows an engineer's original faceplate design reworked by human engineers.

The original concept separated LEDs from their labels, used different labeling scheme for LAN LEDs that caused the user to have to count LEDs to find the number and used a noisy interface. NUREG/CR-1278 estimates errors in selecting the right action in such instances to range from .01 to .001. The convoluted interface was estimated to be in the direction of .01 where as the cleaner interface was expected to perform in the average error range of .003.

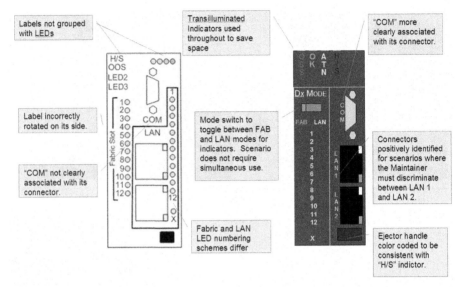

Engineer's Original Concept   Human Engineering Concept

Fig. 4. Bad and Better Human-Machine Interface Design

5 Summary

While engineers strive to make NE so reliable that it does not require maintenance, the reality is that about 50% of all network outages are caused by a human error. These outages are the sum of major design errors, such as the case of reversed wiring and labeling from the normal convention with a quantifiable chance of a total system outage, and the sum of hundreds of minor errors in interface design. The human can be seen as a "black box" in the system with its own coefficients of availability and reliability. In the case where a human is not strong enough to lift a chassis into place, insert or eject a part, the human can be seen as being unavailable, leading to the system being unrepairable. In the case of the interface being confusing, the human is driven to perform his/her duties unreliably.

While the industry as a whole does not gather detailed data for diagnosing the engineering causes of human error, research such as NUREG/CR-1278 indicates that human errors occur as frequently as 1 in 10 items in a checklist from a Method of Procedure and that mistakes like pulling the wrong ejector handle, flipping the wrong breaker or switch, or, disconnecting the wrong cable happen as often as 1 in 100 operations. To counter these error rates, best practice human engineering methods such as those prescribed by the US DoD can be used to great benefit in identifying simple errors on the part of designers that can lead to a simple mistakes. Application of human-factors analysis can resolve current deficiencies in industry standards and lead to a reduction in the likelihood of system outage.

Author Index

Lecture Notes in Computer Science

For information about Vols. 1–4398

please contact your bookseller or Springer

Vol. 4452: M. Fasli, O. Shehory (Eds.), Agent-Mediated Electronic Commerce. VIII, 249 pages. 2007. (Sublibrary LNAI).

Vol. 4451: T.S. Huang, A. Nijholt, M. Pantic, A. Pentland (Eds.), Artifical Intelligence for Human Computing. XVI, 359 pages. 2007. (Sublibrary LNAI).

Vol. 4450: T. Okamoto, X. Wang (Eds.), Public Key Cryptography – PKC 2007. XIII, 491 pages. 2007.

Vol. 4448: M. Giacobini et al. (Ed.), Applications of Evolutionary Computing. XXIII, 755 pages. 2007.

Vol. 4447: E. Marchiori, J.H. Moore, J.C. Rajapakse (Eds.), Evolutionary Computation,Machine Learning and Data Mining in Bioinformatics. XI, 302 pages. 2007.

Vol. 4446: C. Cotta, J. van Hemert (Eds.), Evolutionary Computation in Combinatorial Optimization. XII, 241 pages. 2007.

Vol. 4445: M. Ebner, M. O'Neill, A. Ekárt, L. Vanneschi, A.I. Esparcia-Alcázar (Eds.), Genetic Programming. XI, 382 pages. 2007.

Vol. 4444: T. Reps, M. Sagiv, J. Bauer (Eds.), Program Analysis and Compilation, Theory and Practice. X, 361 pages. 2007.

Vol. 4443: R. Kotagiri, P.R. Krishna, M. Mohania, E. Nantajeewarawat (Eds.), Advances in Databases: Concepts, Systems and Applications. XXI, 1126 pages. 2007.

Vol. 4440: B. Liblit, Cooperative Bug Isolation. XV, 101 pages. 2007.

Vol. 4439: W. Abramowicz (Ed.), Business Information Systems. XV, 654 pages. 2007.

Vol. 4438: L. Maicher, A. Sigel, L.M. Garshol (Eds.), Leveraging the Semantics of Topic Maps. X, 257 pages. 2007. (Sublibrary LNAI).

Vol. 4433: E. Şahin, W.M. Spears, A.F.T. Winfield (Eds.), Swarm Robotics. XII, 221 pages. 2007.

Vol. 4432: B. Beliczynski, A. Dzielinski, M. Iwanowski, B. Ribeiro (Eds.), Adaptive and Natural Computing Algorithms, Part II. XXVI, 761 pages. 2007.

Vol. 4431: B. Beliczynski, A. Dzielinski, M. Iwanowski, B. Ribeiro (Eds.), Adaptive and Natural Computing Algorithms, Part I. XXV, 851 pages. 2007.

Vol. 4430: C.C. Yang, D. Zeng, M. Chau, K. Chang, Q. Yang, X. Cheng, J. Wang, F.-Y. Wang, H. Chen (Eds.), Intelligence and Security Informatics. XII, 330 pages. 2007.

Vol. 4429: R. Lu, J.H. Siekmann, C. Ullrich (Eds.), Cognitive Systems. X, 161 pages. 2007. (Sublibrary LNAI).

Vol. 4427: S. Uhlig, K. Papagiannaki, O. Bonaventure (Eds.), Passive and Active Network Measurement. XI, 274 pages. 2007.

Vol. 4426: Z.-H. Zhou, H. Li, Q. Yang (Eds.), Advances in Knowledge Discovery and Data Mining. XXV, 1161 pages. 2007. (Sublibrary LNAI).

Vol. 4425: G. Amati, C. Carpineto, G. Romano (Eds.), Advances in Information Retrieval. XIX, 759 pages. 2007.

Vol. 4424: O. Grumberg, M. Huth (Eds.), Tools and Algorithms for the Construction and Analysis of Systems. XX, 738 pages. 2007.

Vol. 4423: H. Seidl (Ed.), Foundations of Software Science and Computational Structures. XVI, 379 pages. 2007.

Vol. 4422: M.B. Dwyer, A. Lopes (Eds.), Fundamental Approaches to Software Engineering. XV, 440 pages. 2007.

Vol. 4421: R. De Nicola (Ed.), Programming Languages and Systems. XVII, 538 pages. 2007.

Vol. 4420: S. Krishnamurthi, M. Odersky (Eds.), Compiler Construction. XIV, 233 pages. 2007.

Vol. 4419: P.C. Diniz, E. Marques, K. Bertels, M.M. Fernandes, J.M.P. Cardoso (Eds.), Reconfigurable Computing: Architectures, Tools and Applications. XIV, 391 pages. 2007.

Vol. 4418: A. Gagalowicz, W. Philips (Eds.), Computer Vision/Computer Graphics Collaboration Techniques. XV, 620 pages. 2007.

Vol. 4416: A. Bemporad, A. Bicchi, G. Buttazzo (Eds.), Hybrid Systems: Computation and Control. XVII, 797 pages. 2007.

Vol. 4415: P. Lukowicz, L. Thiele, G. Tröster (Eds.), Architecture of Computing Systems - ARCS 2007. X, 297 pages. 2007.

Vol. 4414: S. Hochreiter, R. Wagner (Eds.), Bioinformatics Research and Development. XVI, 482 pages. 2007. (Sublibrary LNBI).

Vol. 4412: F. Stajano, H.J. Kim, J.-S. Chae, S.-D. Kim (Eds.), Ubiquitous Convergence Technology. XI, 302 pages. 2007.

Vol. 4411: R.H. Bordini, M. Dastani, J. Dix, A.E.F. Seghrouchni (Eds.), Programming Multi-Agent Systems. XIV, 249 pages. 2007. (Sublibrary LNAI).

Vol. 4410: A. Branco (Ed.), Anaphora: Analysis, Algorithms and Applications. X, 191 pages. 2007. (Sublibrary LNAI).

Vol. 4409: J.L. Fiadeiro, P.-Y. Schobbens (Eds.), Recent Trends in Algebraic Development Techniques. VII, 171 pages. 2007.

Vol. 4407: G. Puebla (Ed.), Logic-Based Program Synthesis and Transformation. VIII, 237 pages. 2007.

Vol. 4406: W. De Meuter (Ed.), Advances in Smalltalk. VII, 157 pages. 2007.

Vol. 4405: L. Padgham, F. Zambonelli (Eds.), Agent-Oriented Software Engineering VII. XII, 225 pages. 2007.

Vol. 4403: S. Obayashi, K. Deb, C. Poloni, T. Hiroyasu, T. Murata (Eds.), Evolutionary Multi-Criterion Optimization. XIX, 954 pages. 2007.

Vol. 4401: N. Guelfi, D. Buchs (Eds.), Rapid Integration of Software Engineering Techniques. IX, 177 pages. 2007.

Vol. 4400: J.F. Peters, A. Skowron, V.W. Marek, E. Orłowska, R. Słowiński, W. Ziarko (Eds.), Transactions on Rough Sets VII, Part II. X, 381 pages. 2007.

Vol. 4399: T. Kovacs, X. Llorà, K. Takadama, P.L. Lanzi, W. Stolzmann, S.W. Wilson (Eds.), Learning Classifier Systems. XII, 345 pages. 2007. (Sublibrary LNAI).